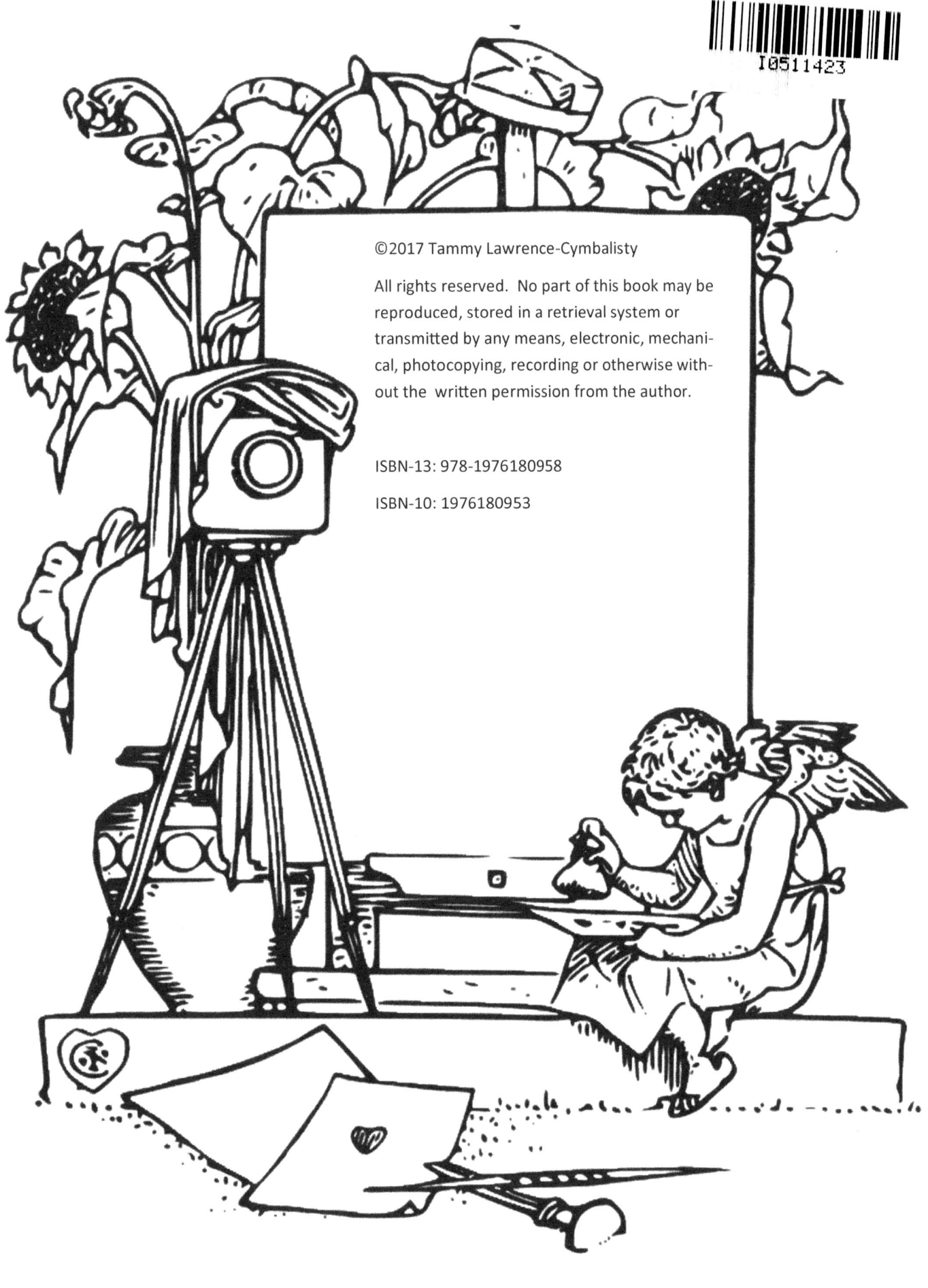

©2017 Tammy Lawrence-Cymbalisty

All rights reserved. No part of this book may be reproduced, stored in a retrieval system or transmitted by any means, electronic, mechanical, photocopying, recording or otherwise without the written permission from the author.

ISBN-13: 978-1976180958

ISBN-10: 1976180953

Welcome to My Chinese Zodiac Colouring Book: All 12 signs. This is a compilation of the artwork featured in our Chinese Zodiac Colouring Books. You'll find 3 pictures of each of the Chinese Zodiac signs featured in our other books.

Thank you so much for your purchase!

Each sign holds different themes to their personality. These themes and characteristics are said to be based on the elements. You'll find some of them listed in the final pages of this book along with a meditation to help you further connect with your Zodiac Animal. Here are the years for each Zodiac Animal:

Rat: 2008, 1996, 1984, 1972, 1960, 1948

Ox: 2009, 1997, 1985, 1973, 1961, 1949

Tiger: 2010, 1998, 1986, 1974, 1962, 1950

Rabbit: 2011, 1999, 1987, 1975, , 1951, 1939

Dragon: 2012, 2000, 1988, 1976, 1964, 1952, 1940

Snake: 2013, 2001, 1989, 1977, 1965, 1953, 1941

Horse: 2014, 2002, 1990, 1978, 1966, 1954, 1942

Goat/Ram/Sheep: 2015, 2003, 1991, 1979, 1967, 1955, 1943

Monkey: 2016, 2004, 1992, 1980, 1968, 1956, 1944

Rooster: 2017, 2005, 1993, 1981, 1969, 1957, 1945

Dog: 2018, 2006, 1994, 1982, 1970, 1958, 1946

Pig: 2019, 2007, 1995, 1983, 1971, 1959, 1947

I suggest placing a piece of paper behind the pictures (you could also choose waxed paper) to prevent bleed-through. The pictures have a page between them to help with this.

You'll find lots of areas in the pictures to add further creations. For example you could turn it into a journal by writing about your day in the blank areas, play with some interesting fonts or add your favourite affirmations; build on what you find here. You are the artist so whatever you create will be perfect!

Happy colouring!

Wishing you many continued blessings,

Tammy

My Chinese Zodiac Colouring Book series:

I'm a Horse: My Chinese Zodiac Colouring Book

I'm the Monkey: My Chinese Zodiac Colouring Book

I'm a Goat: Year of the Goat (Sheep or Ram)

I'm a Dog: My Chinese Zodiac Colouring Book

I'm an Ox: Year of the Ox

I'm a Pig: Year of the Pig

I'm a Rat: Year of the Rat

I'm a Rabbit: My Chinese Zodiac Colouring Book

I'm a Snake: My Chinese Zodiac Colouring Book

I'm a Dragon: Year of the Dragon

I'm a Tiger: Year of the Tiger

I'm a Rooster: Year of the Rooster

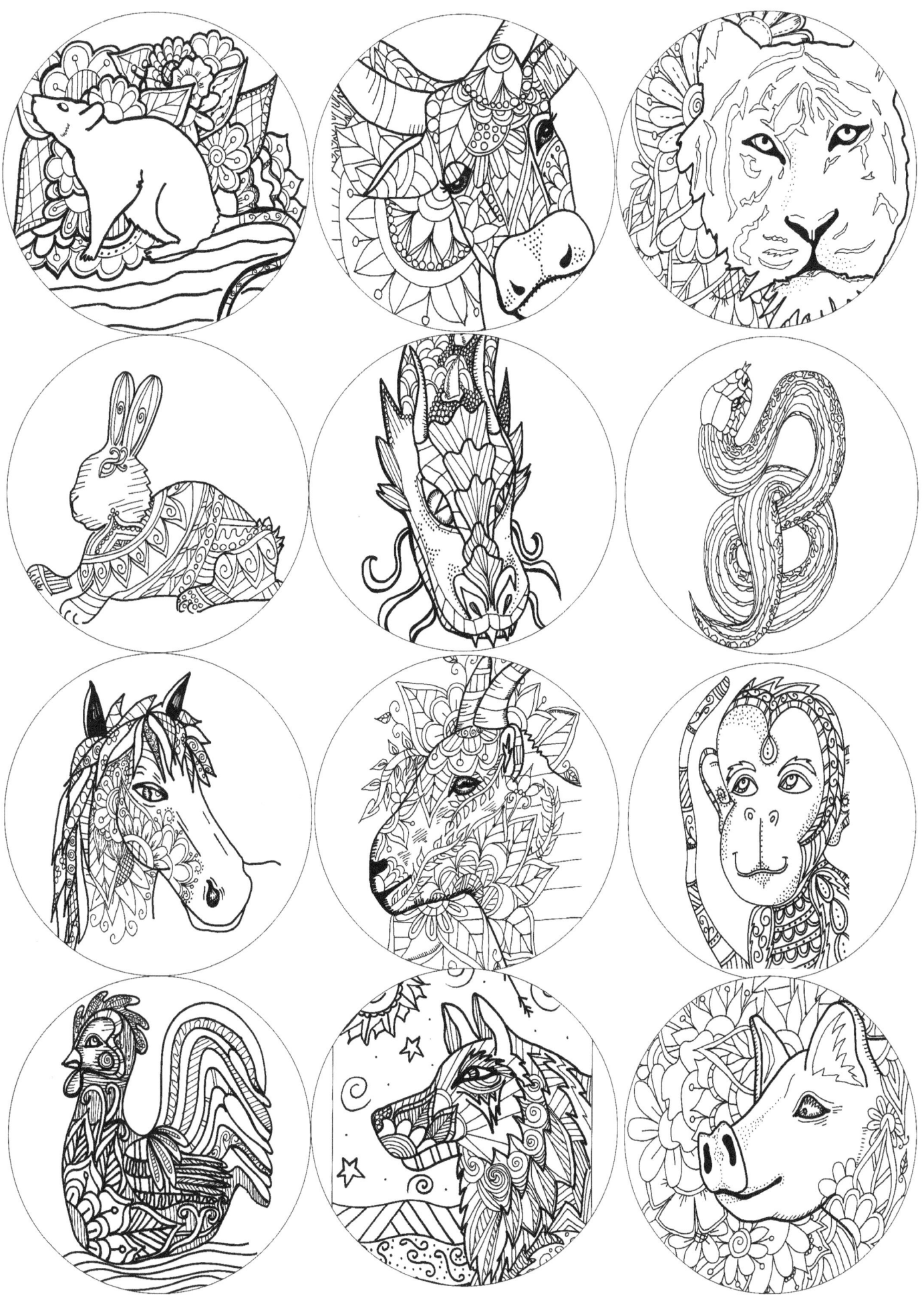

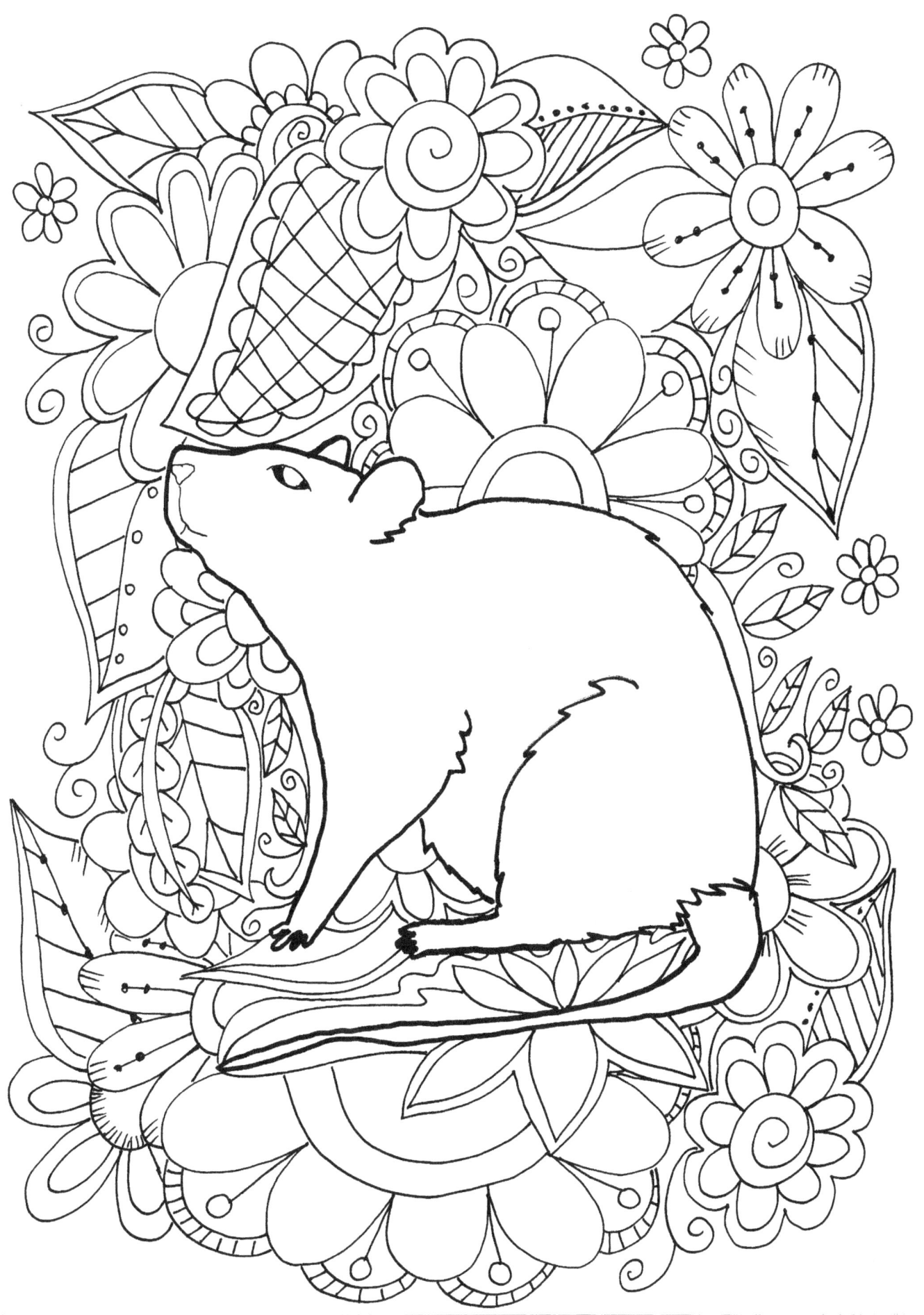

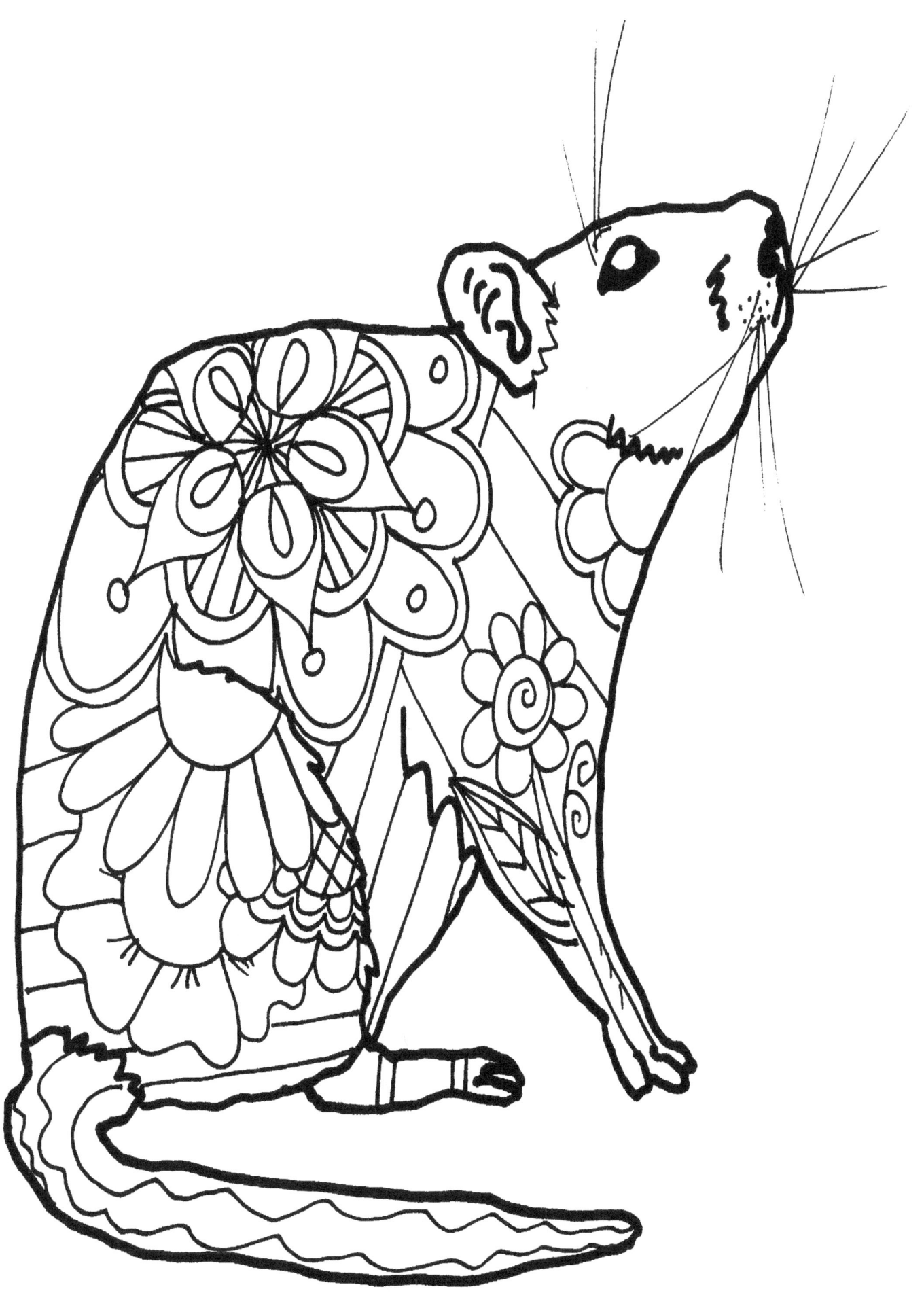

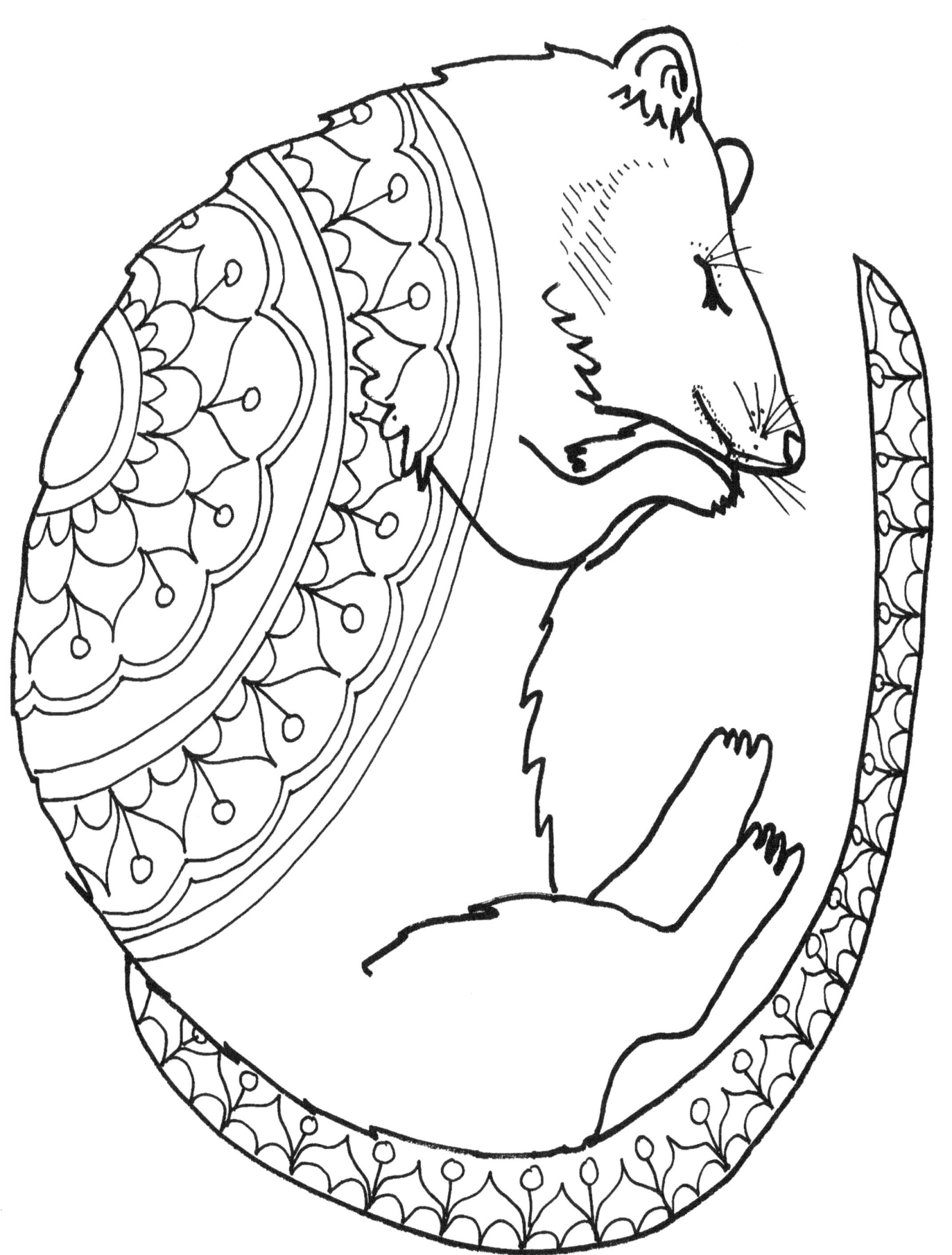

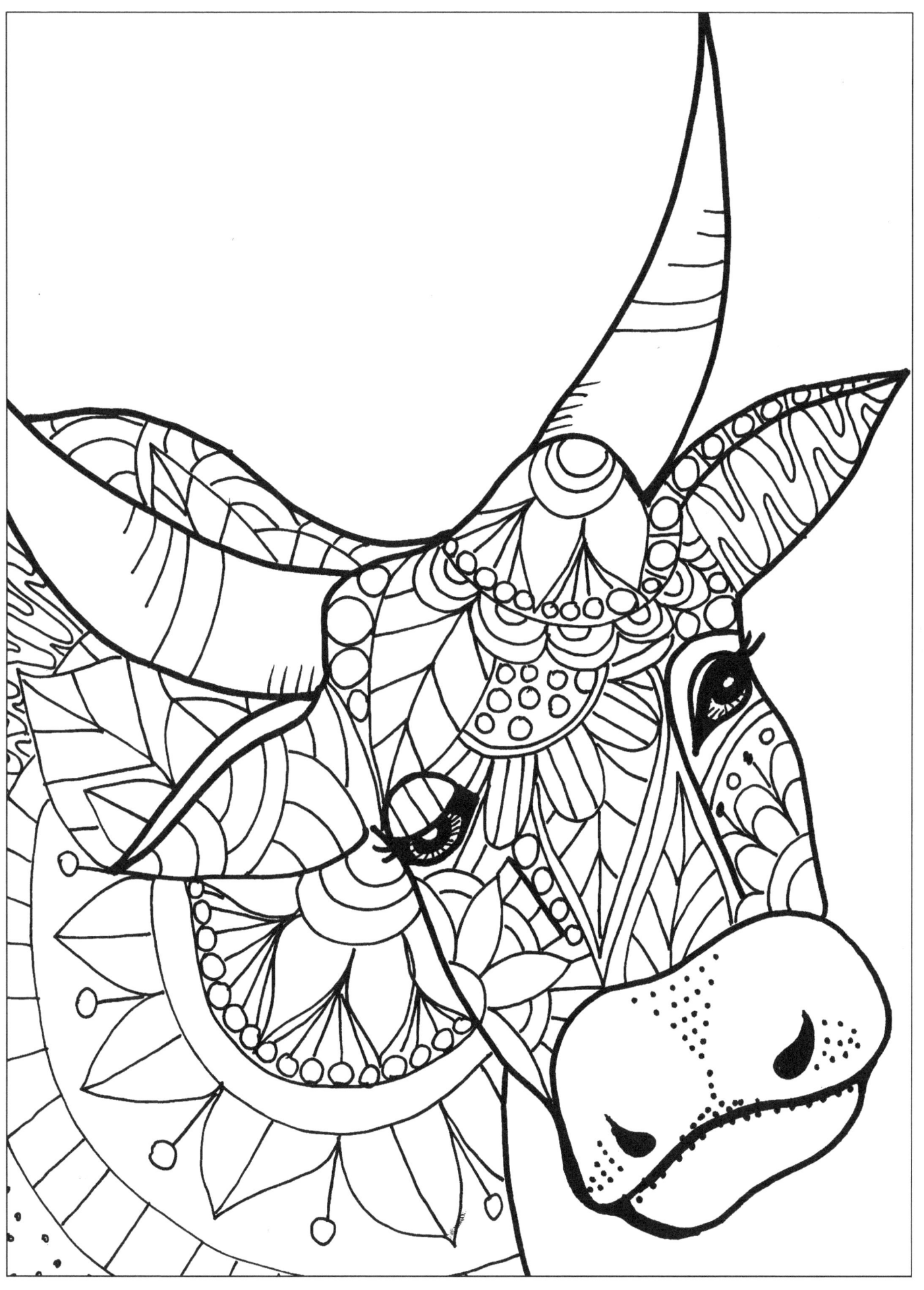

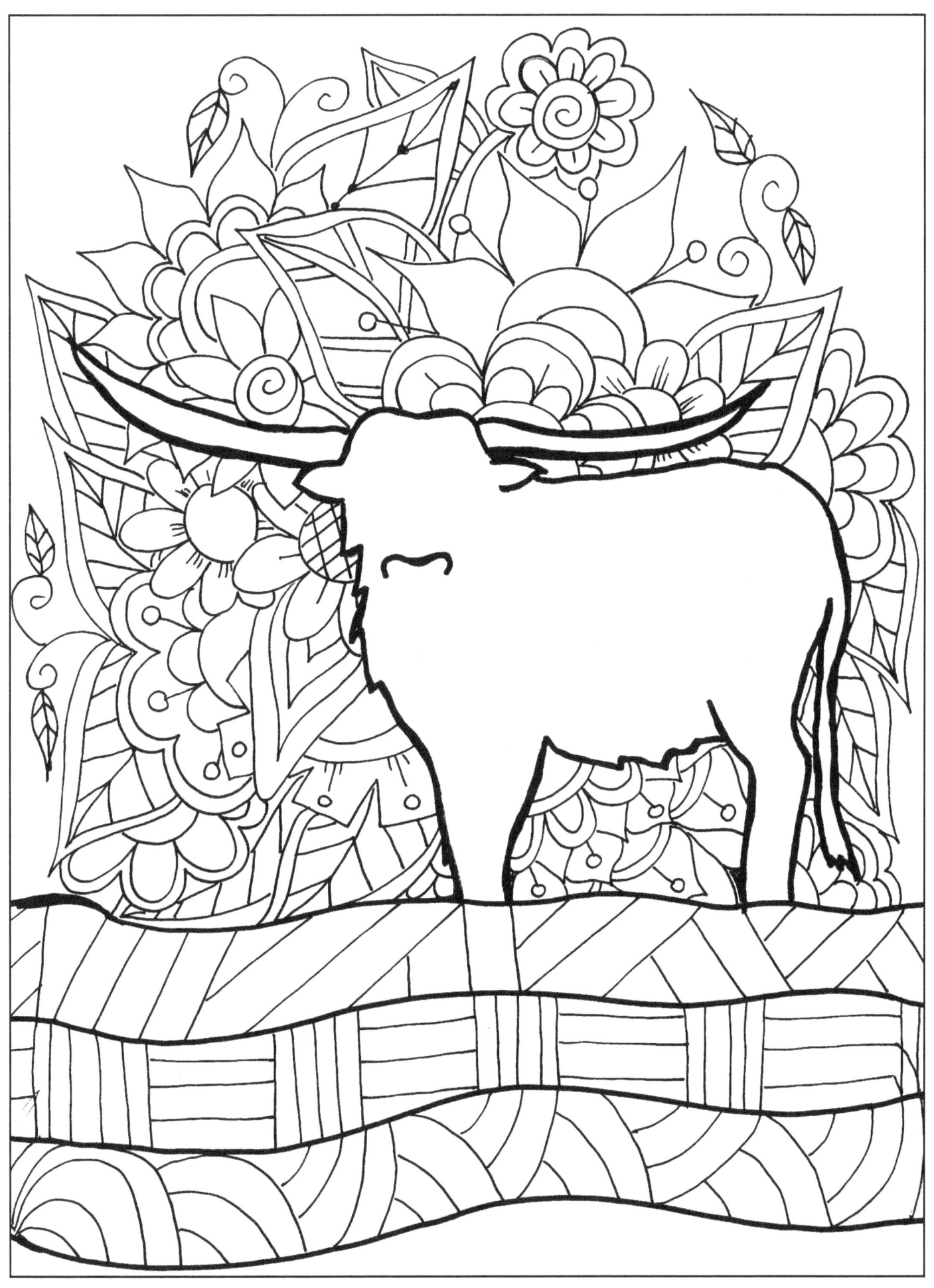

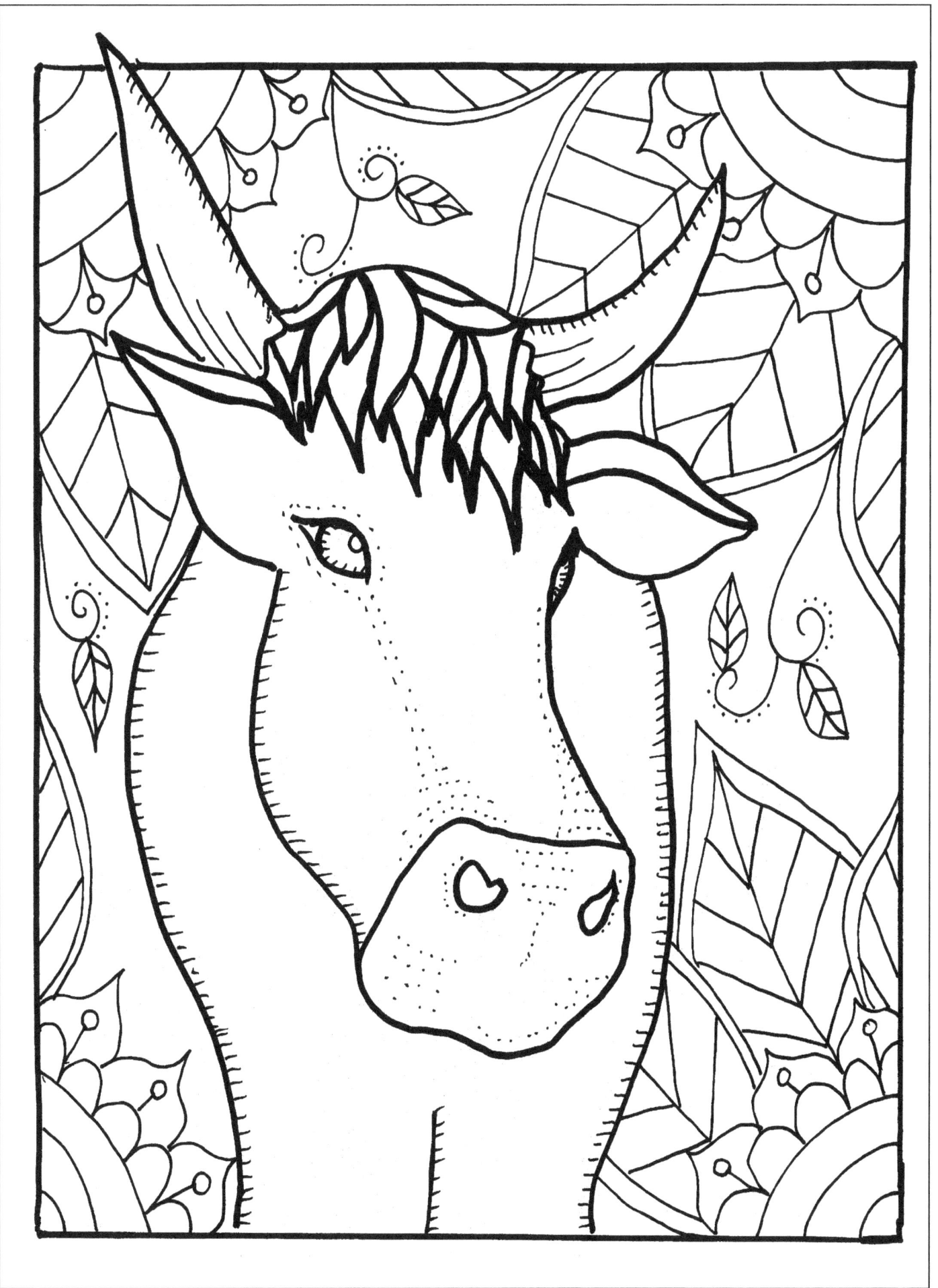

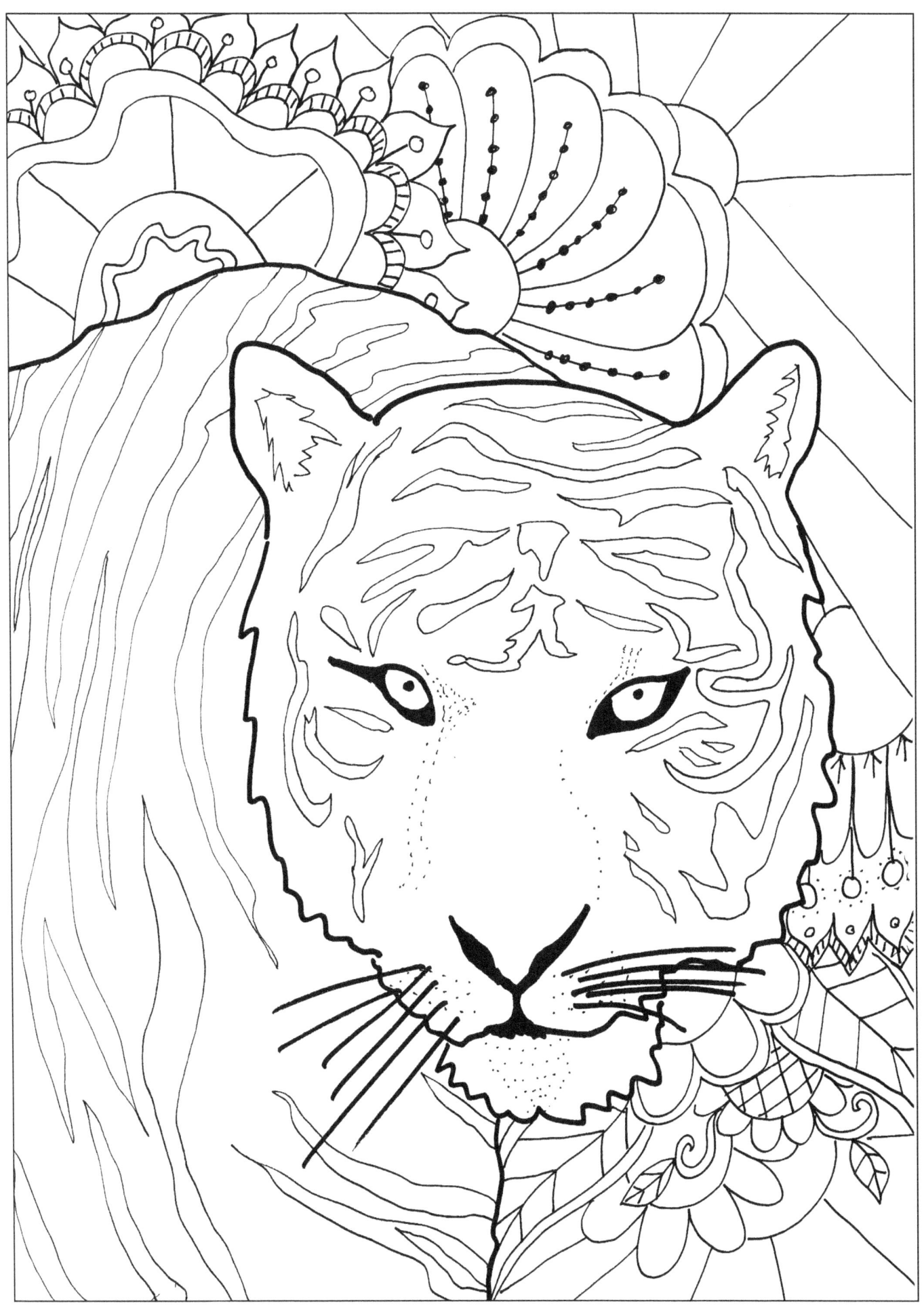

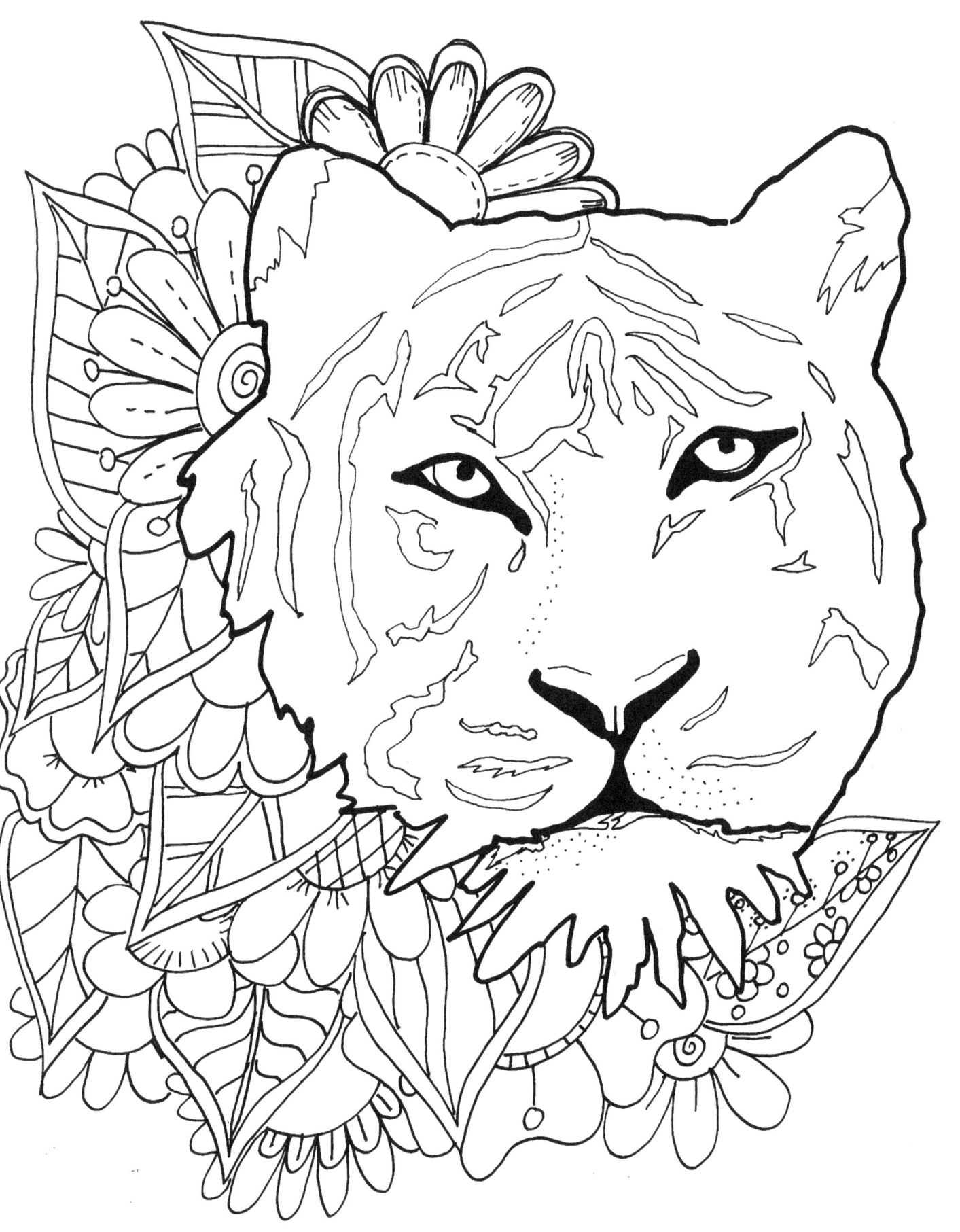

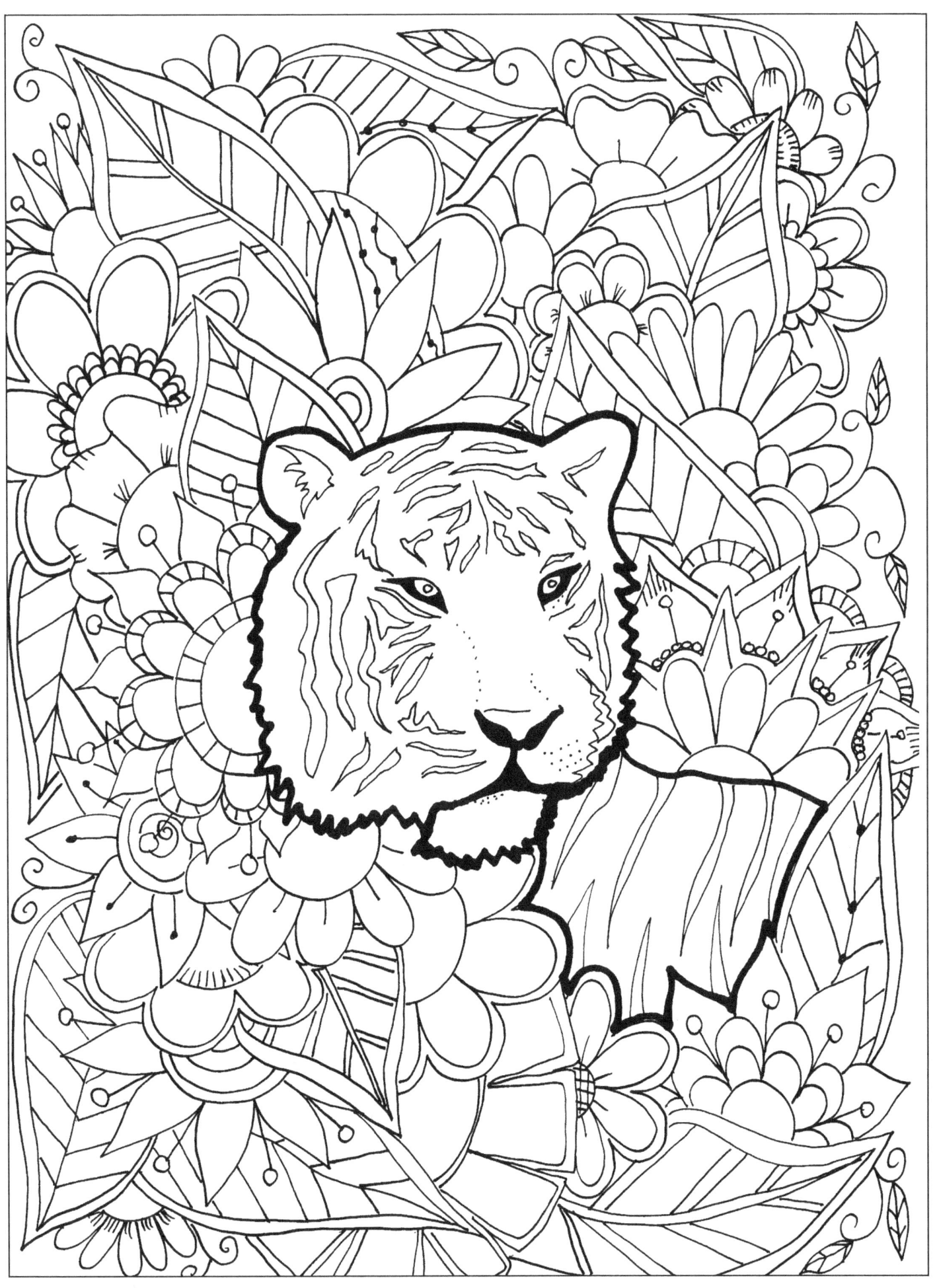

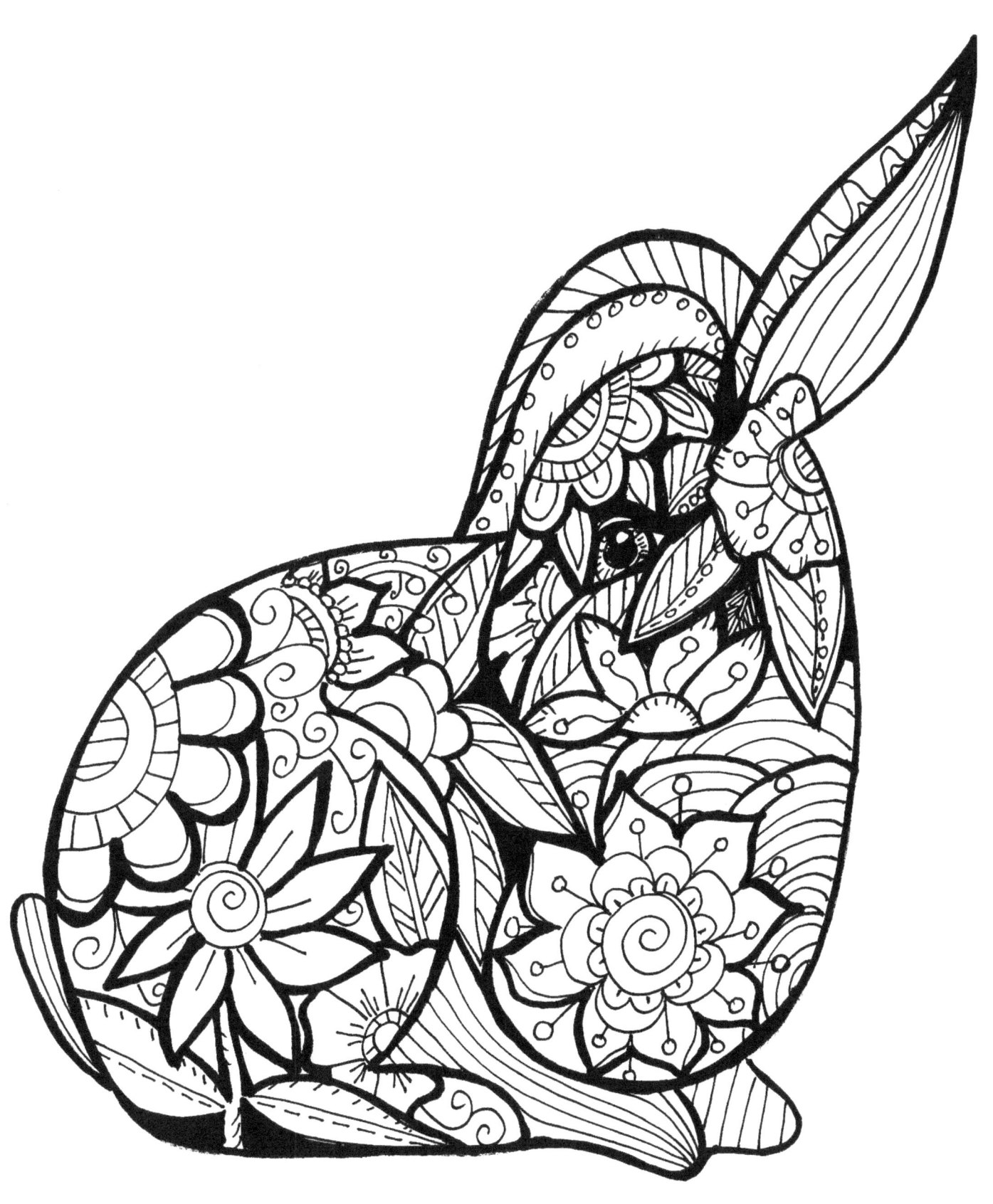

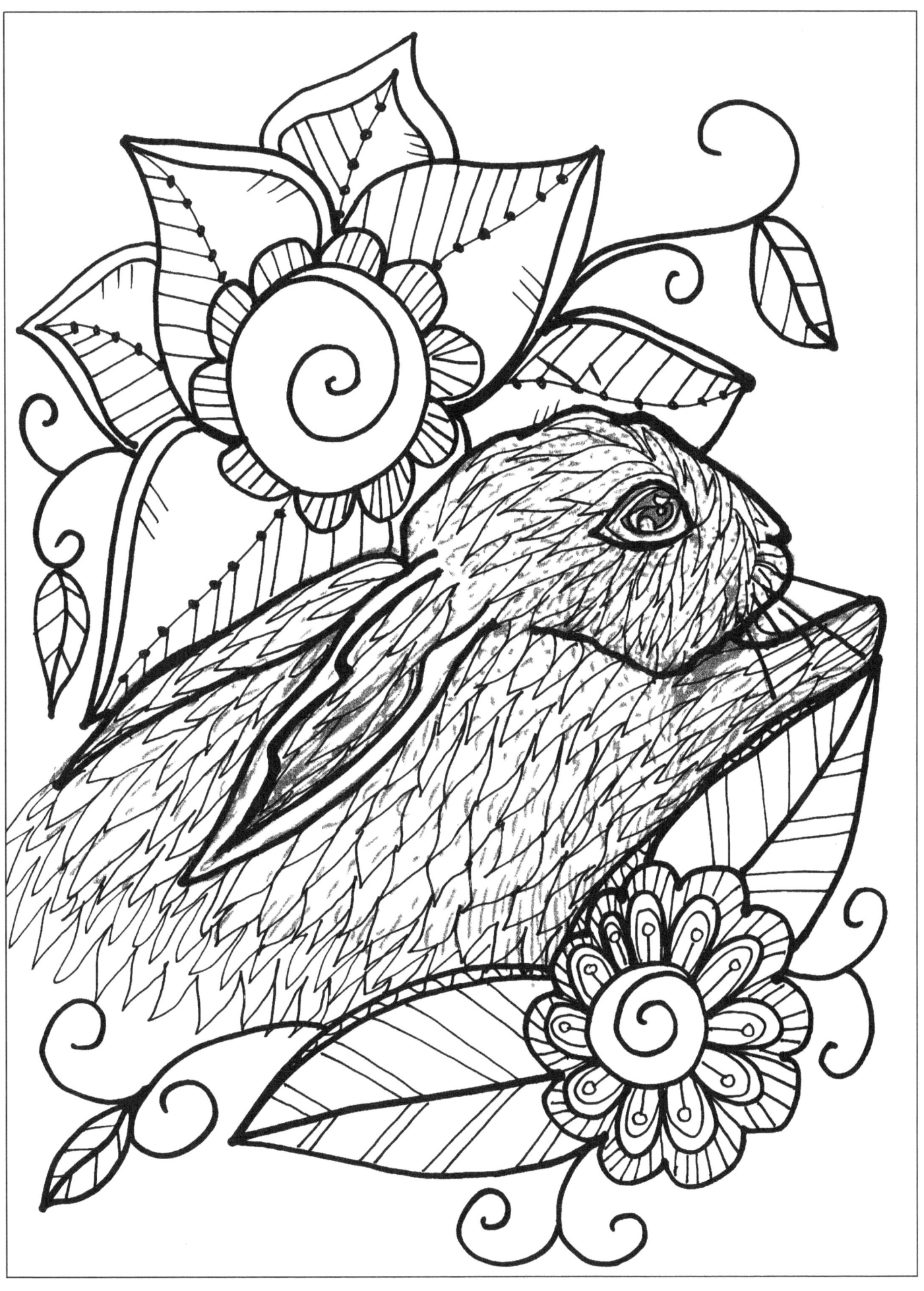

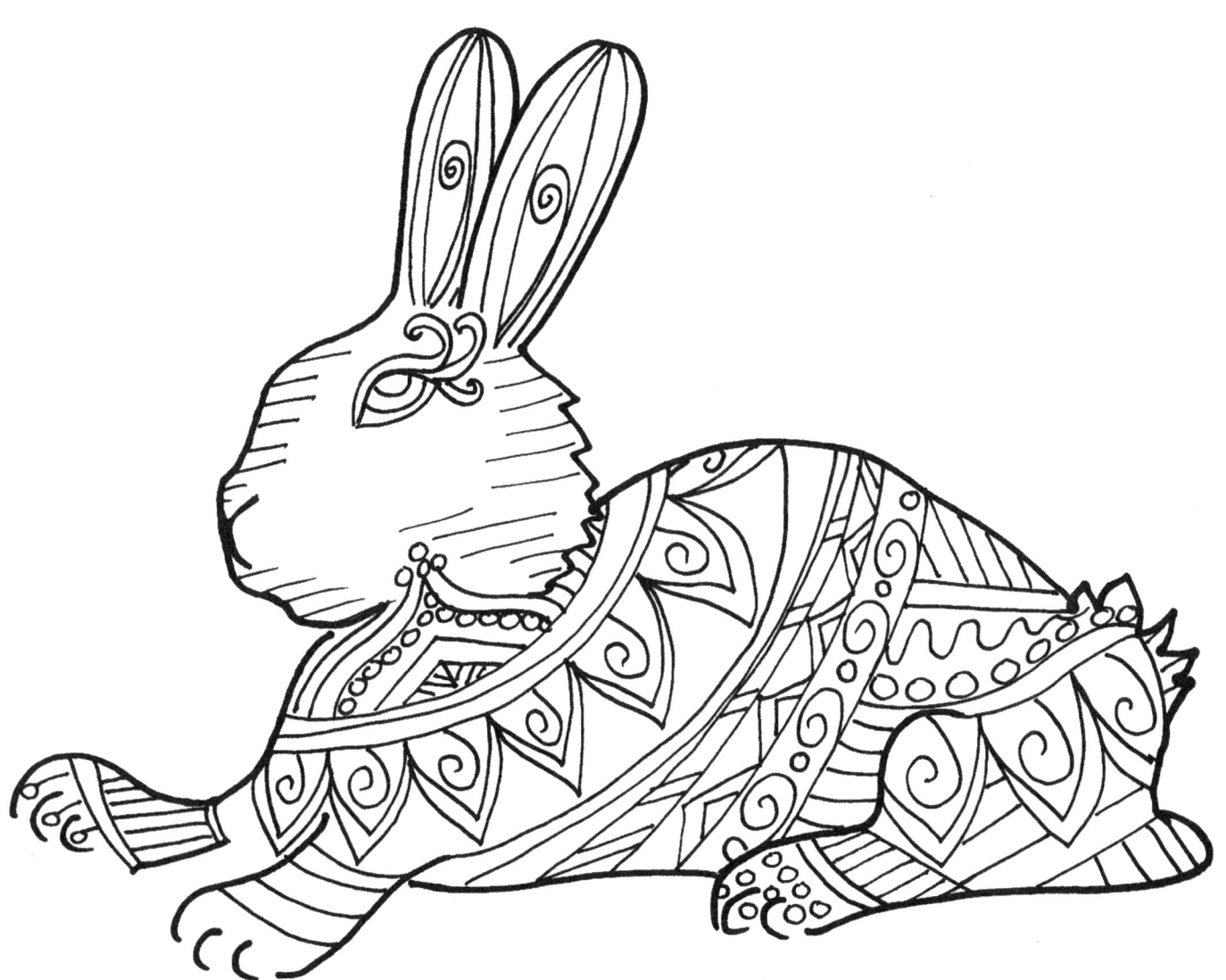

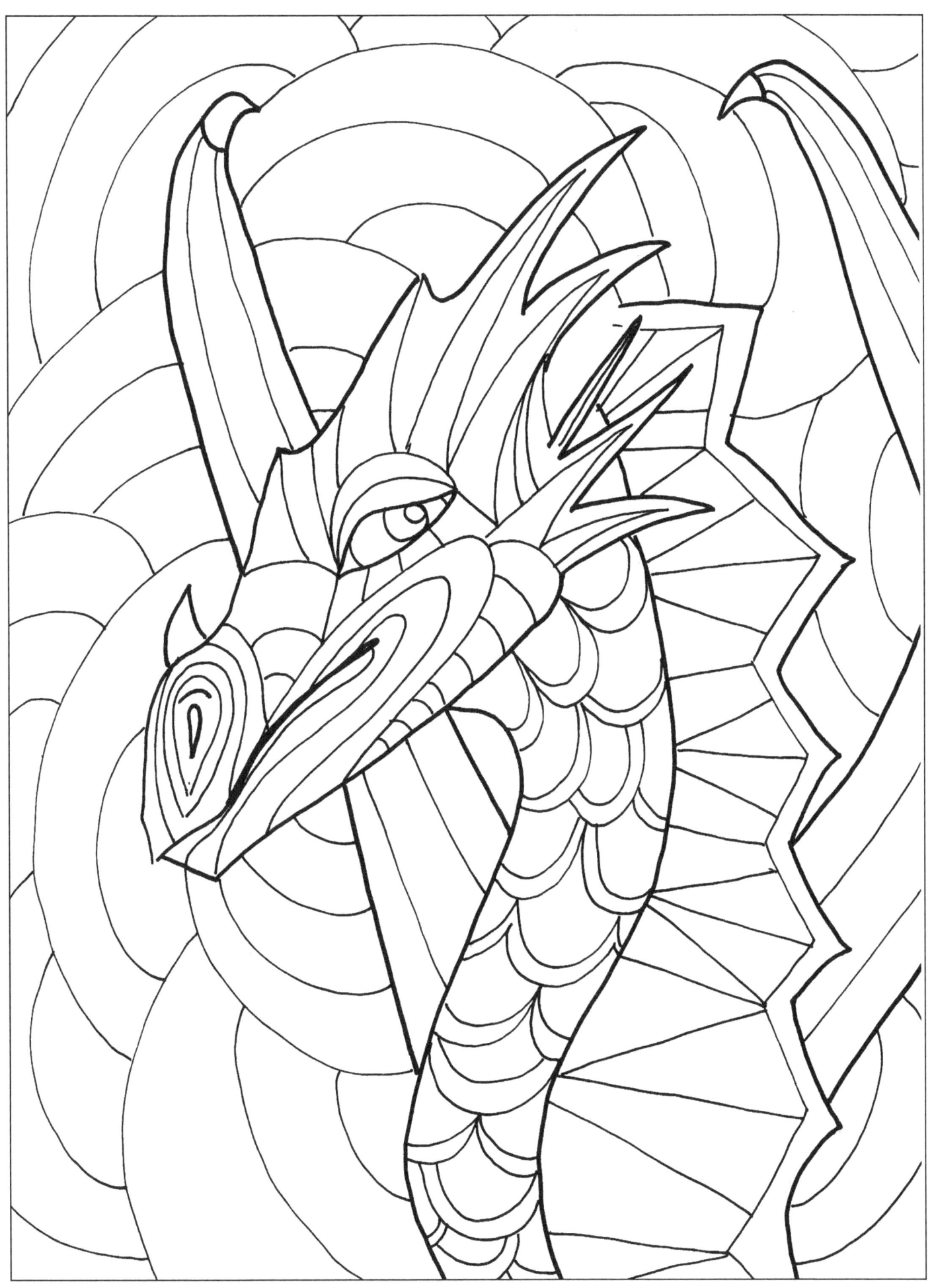

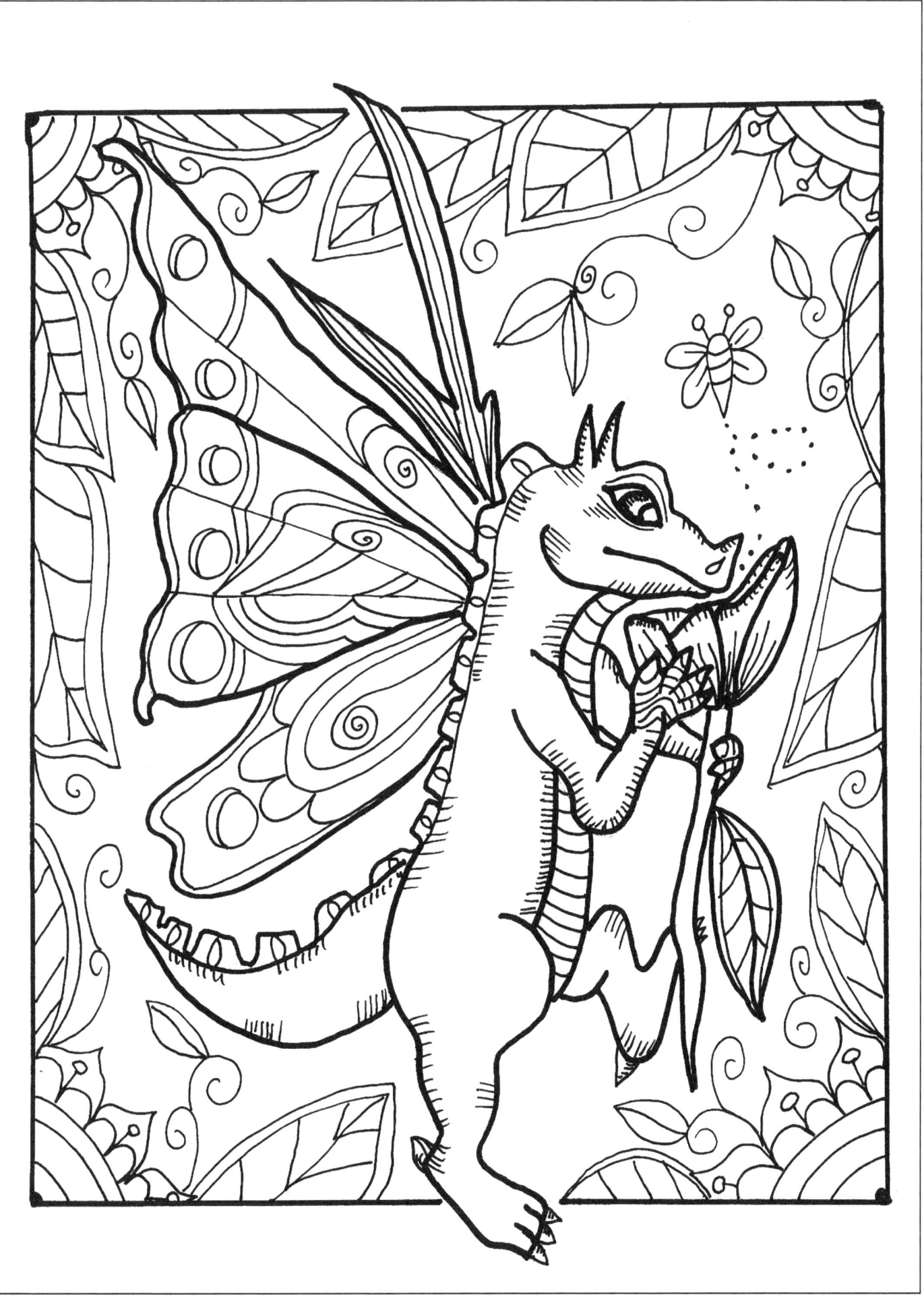

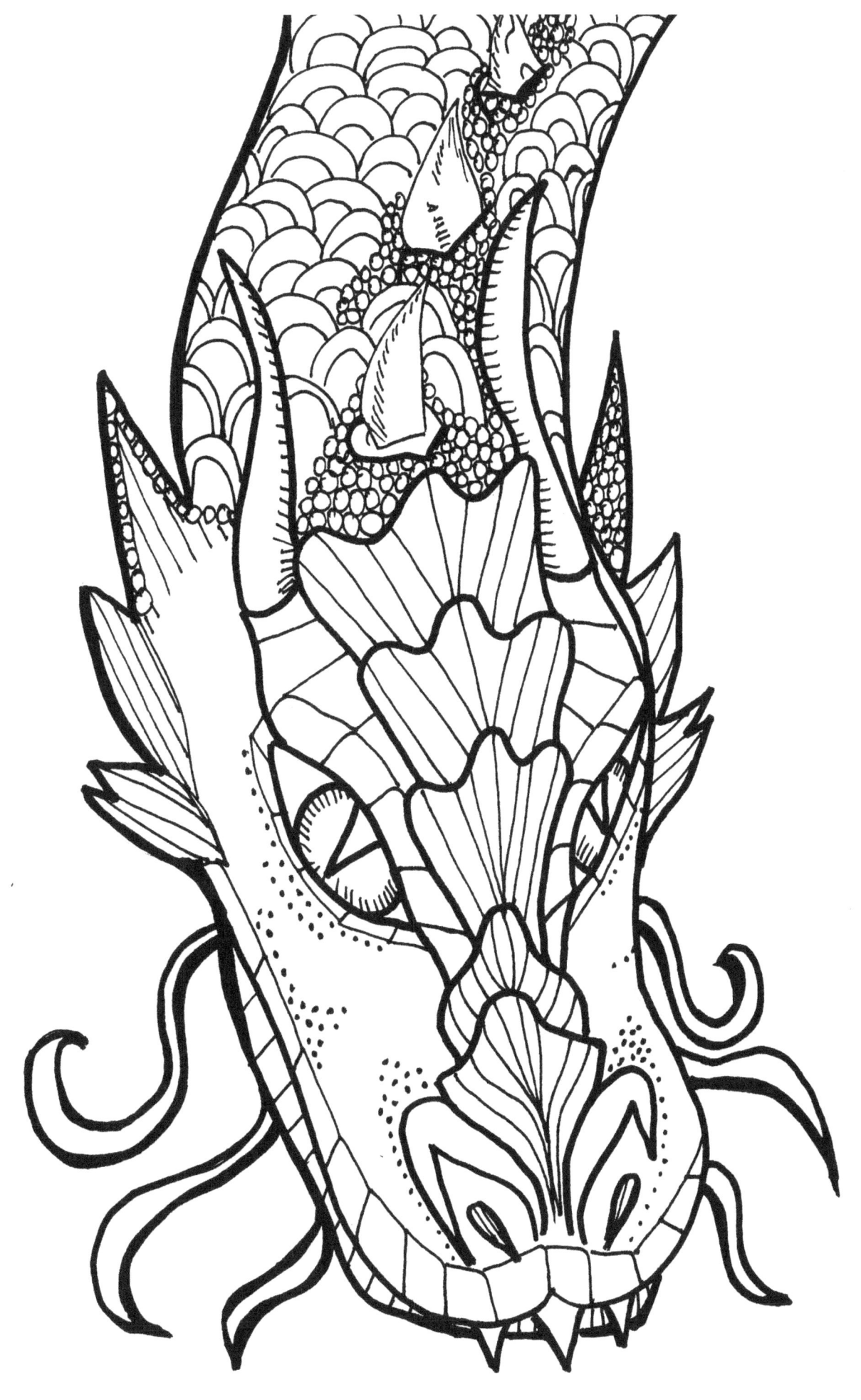

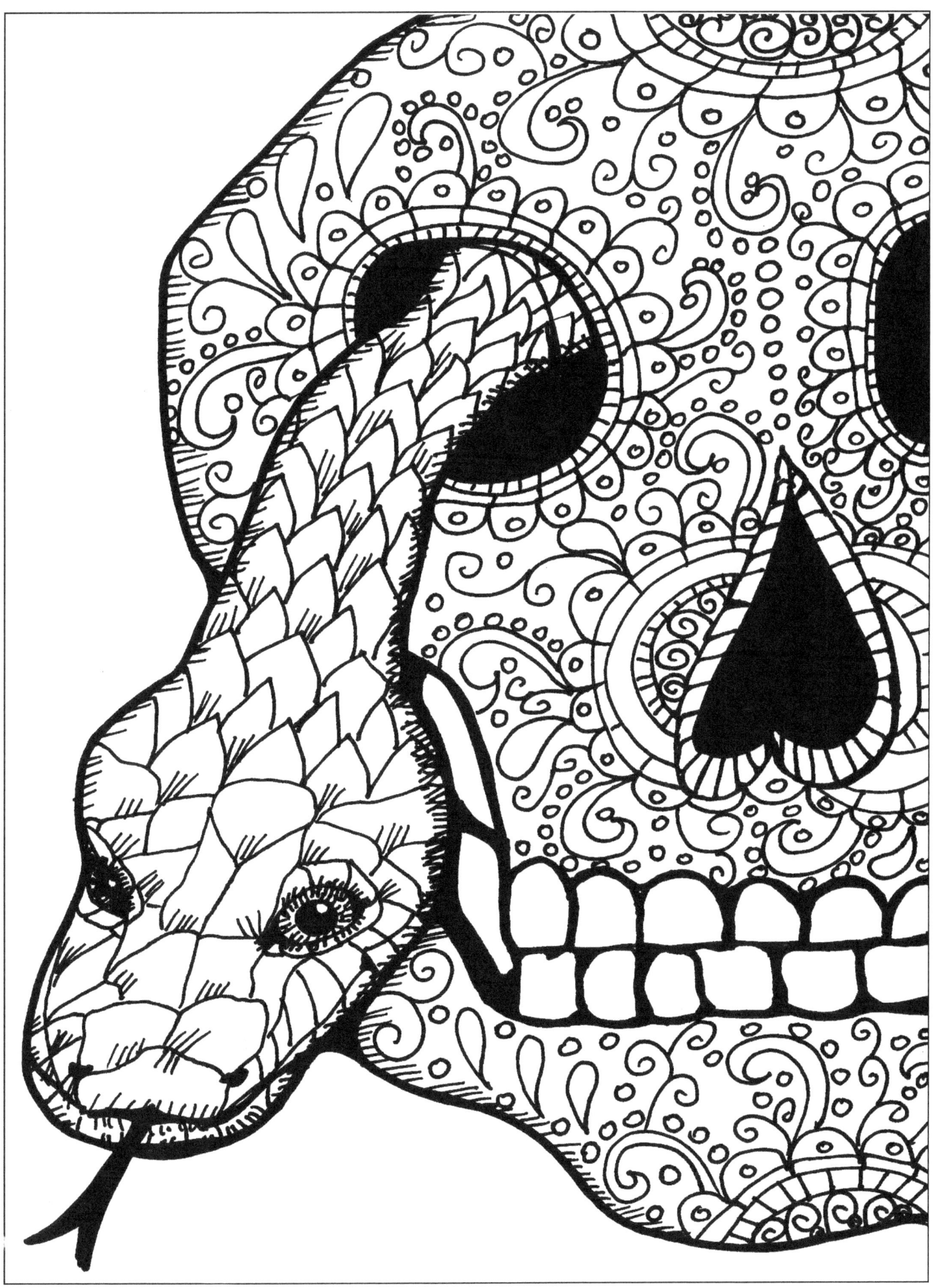

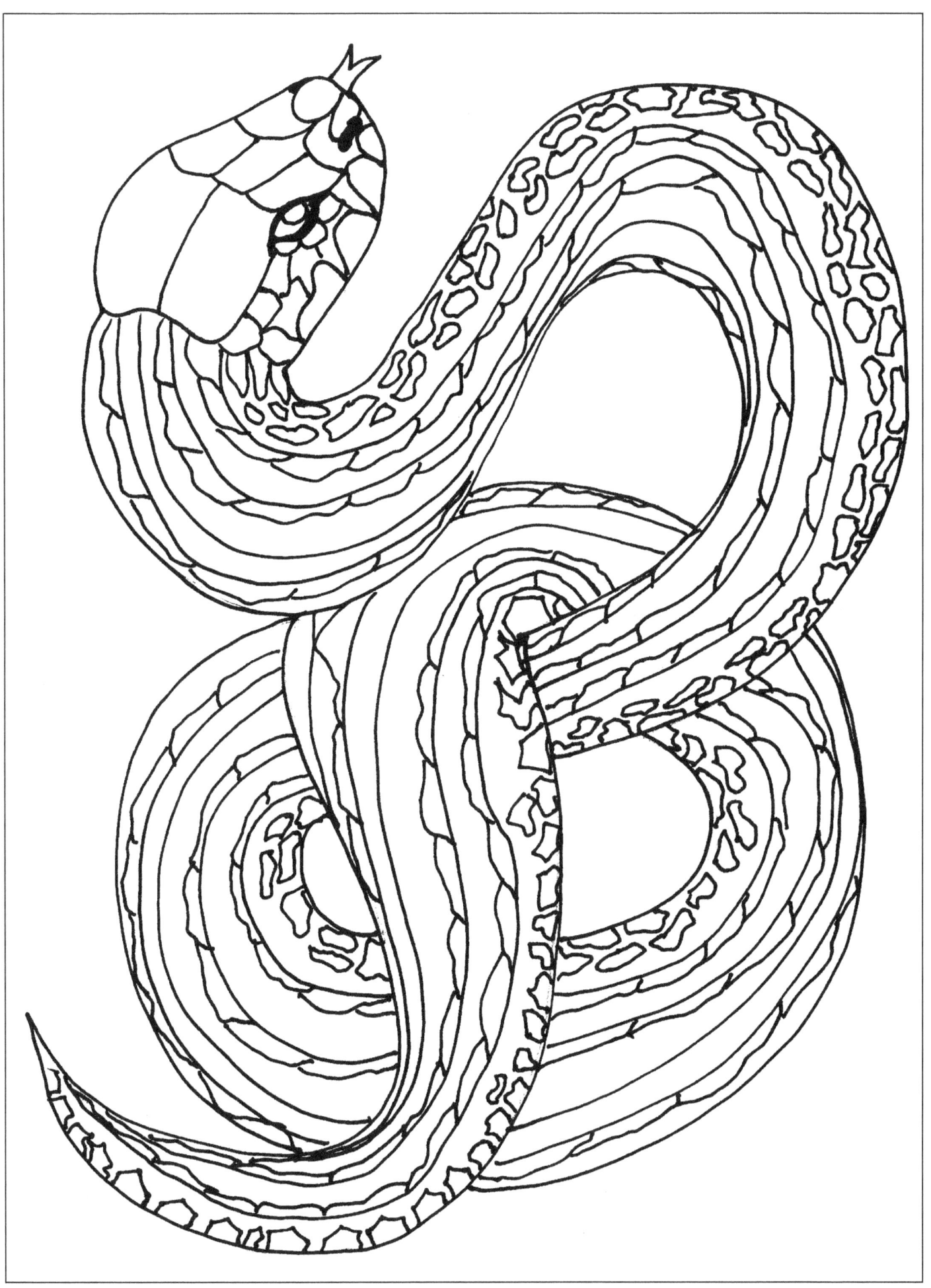

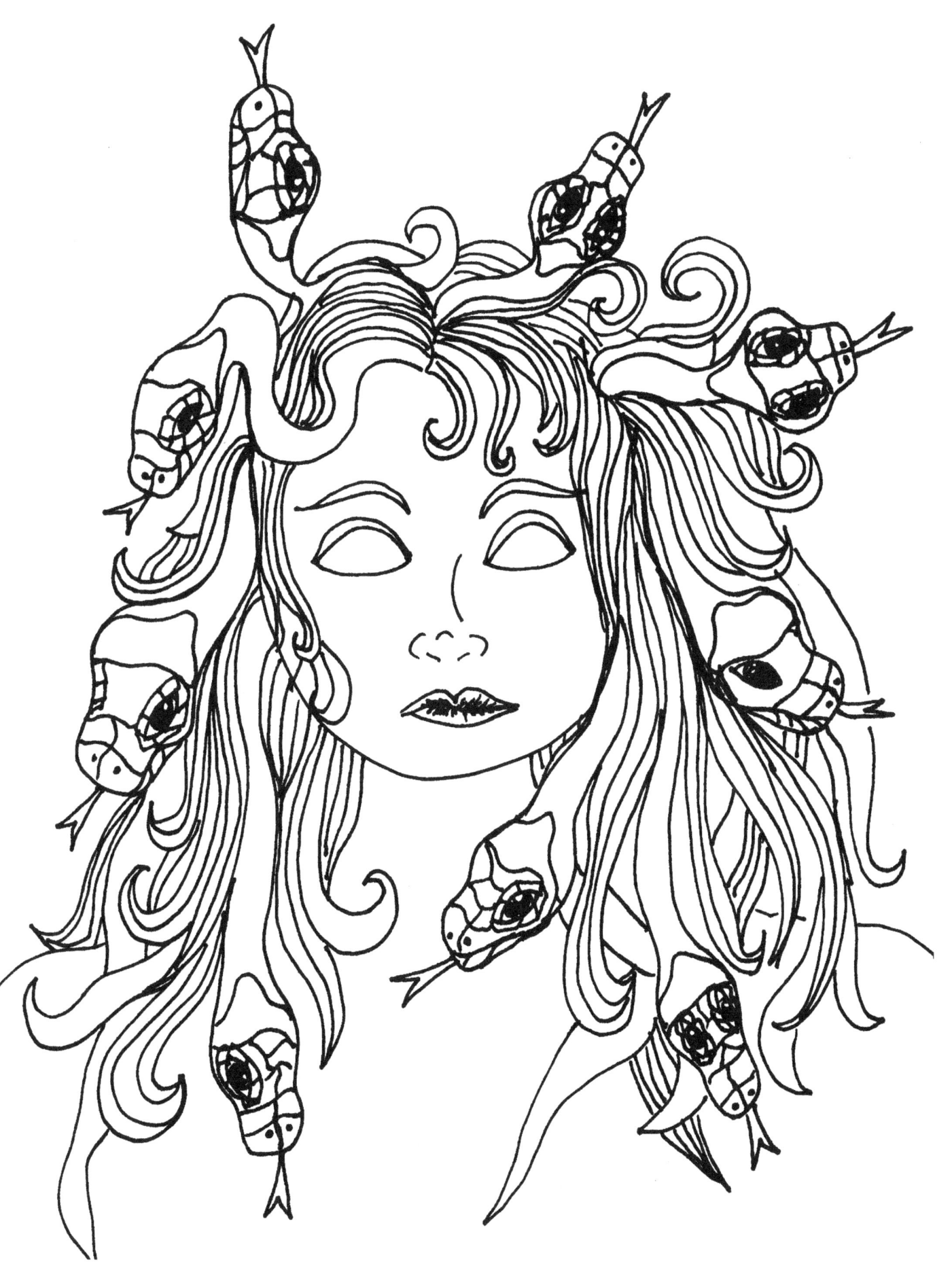

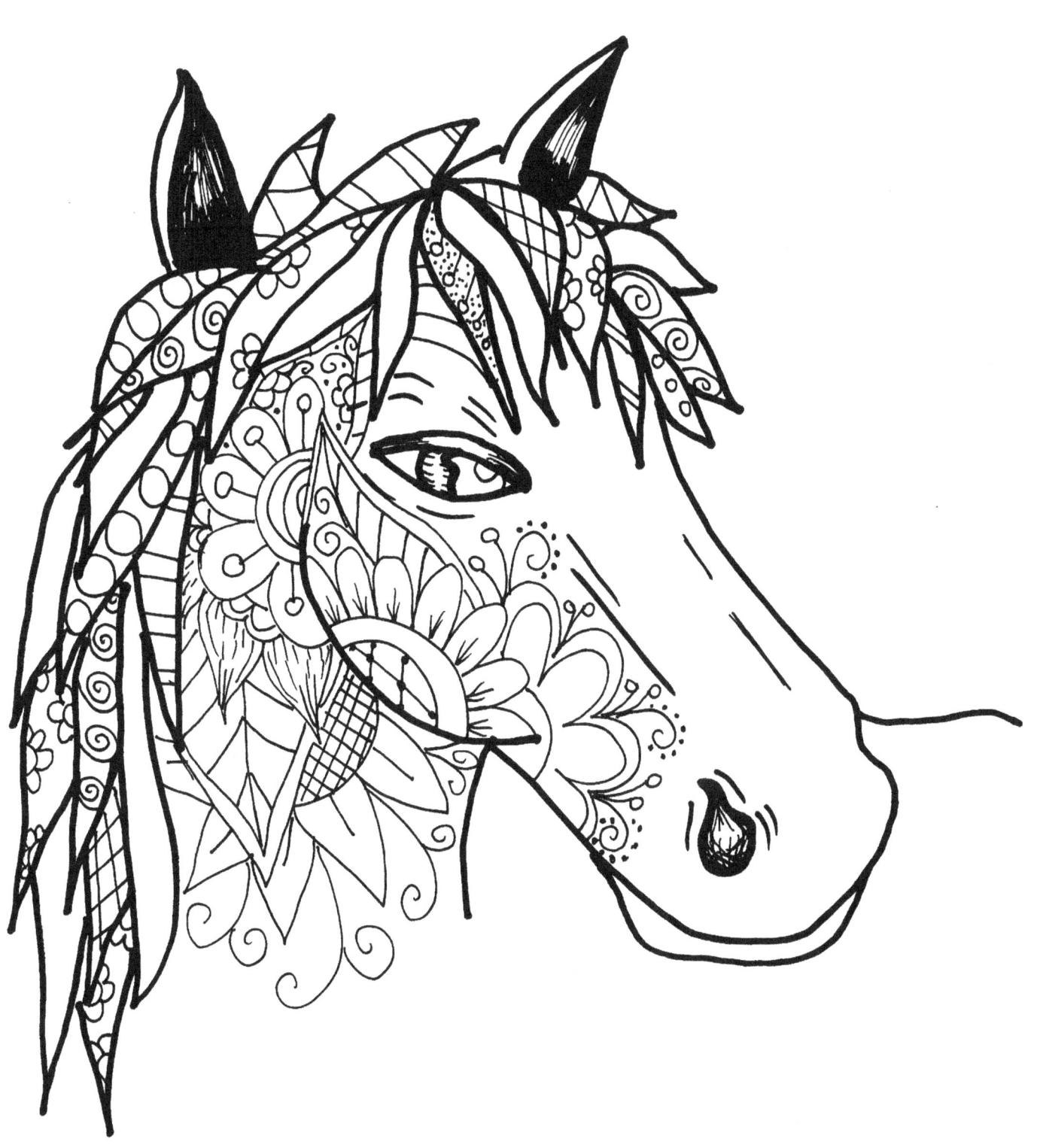

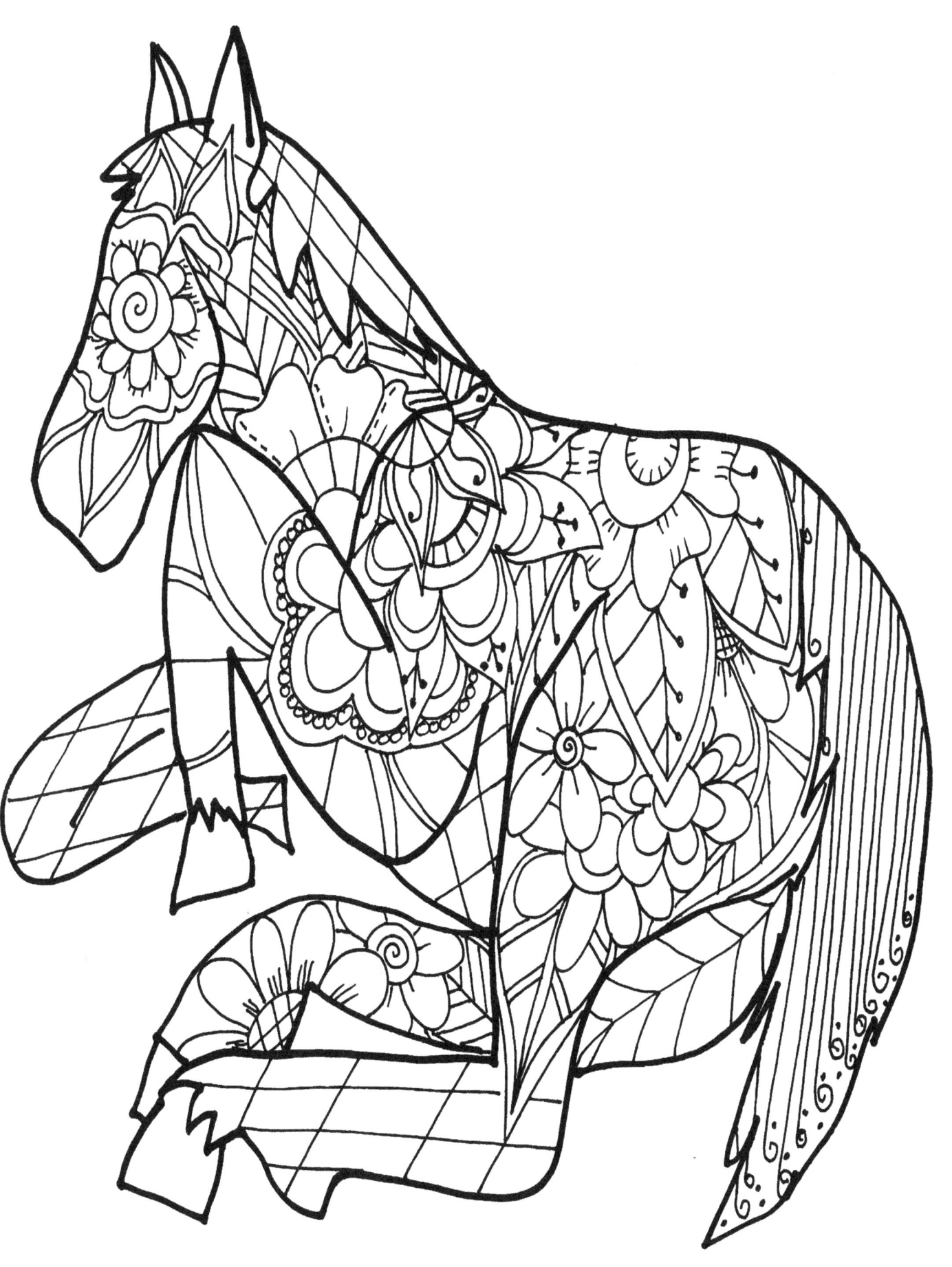

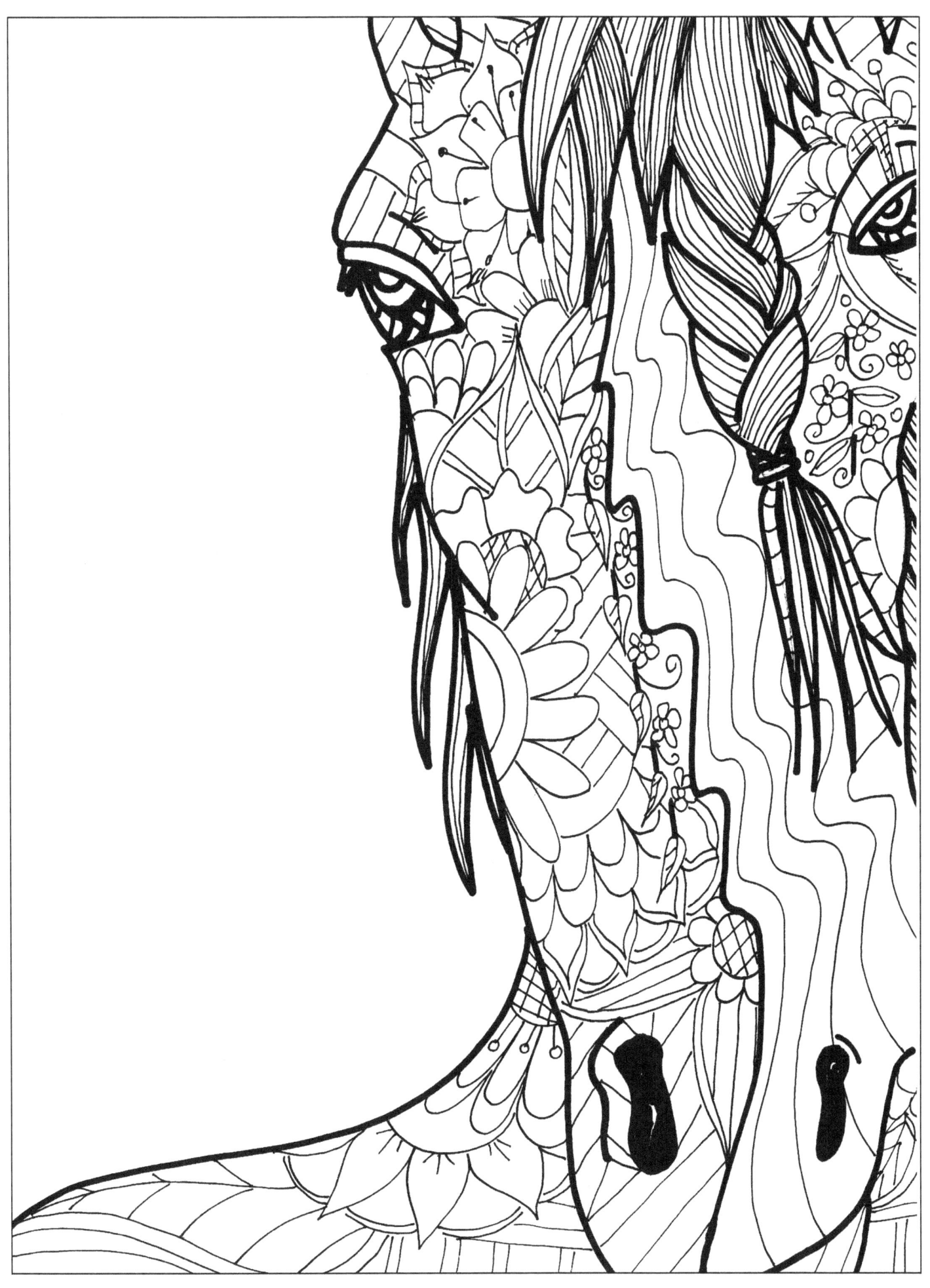

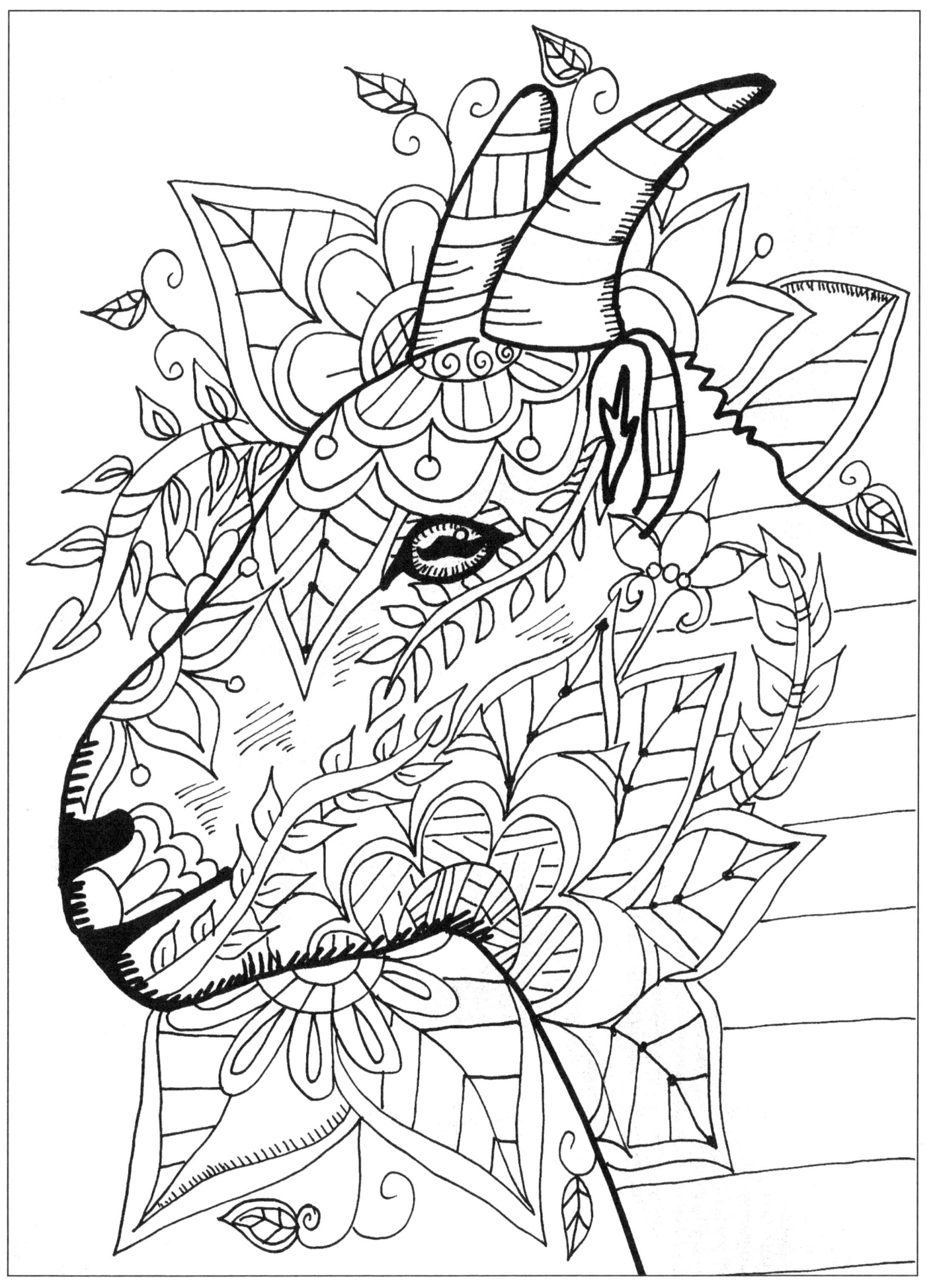

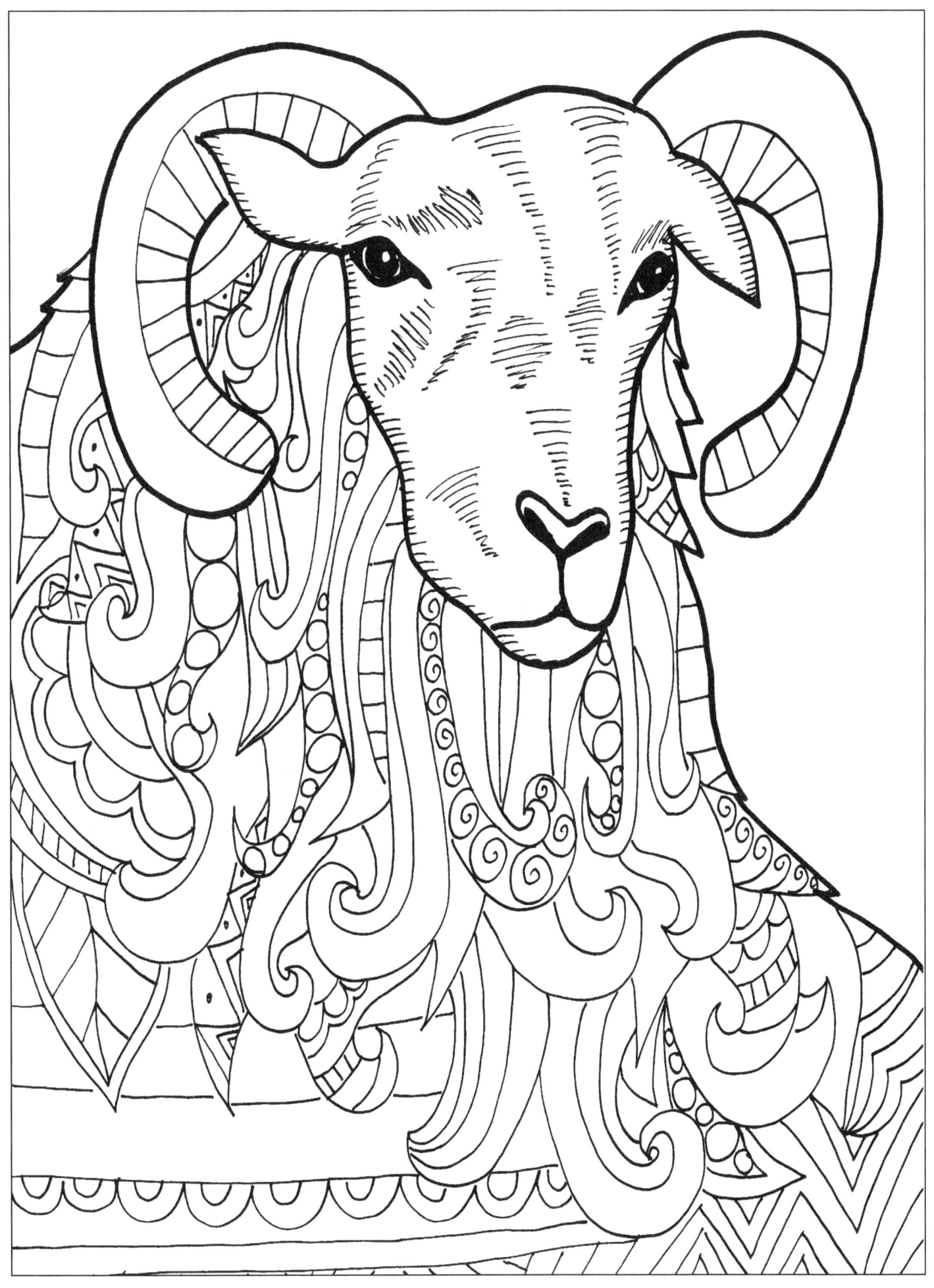

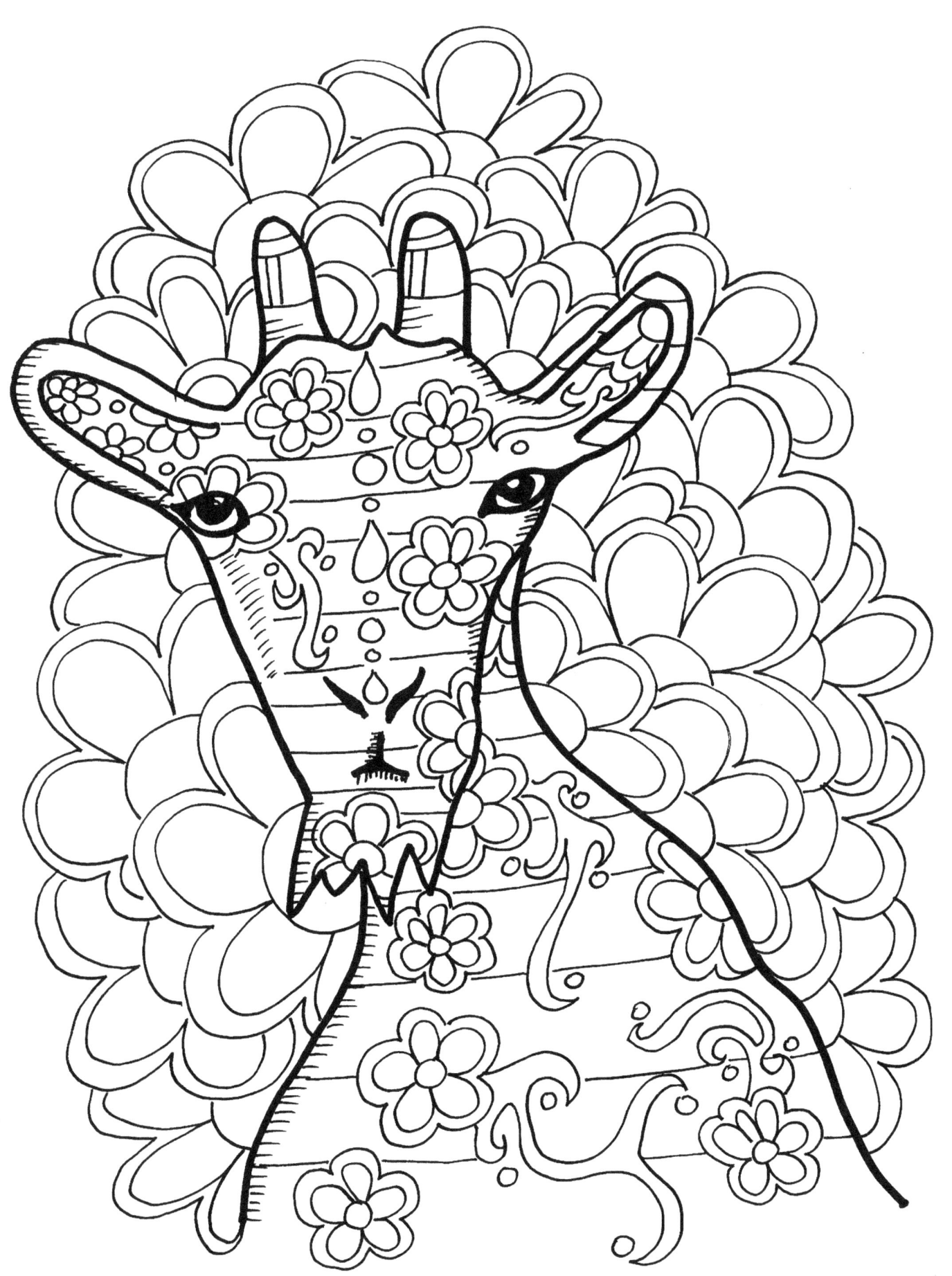

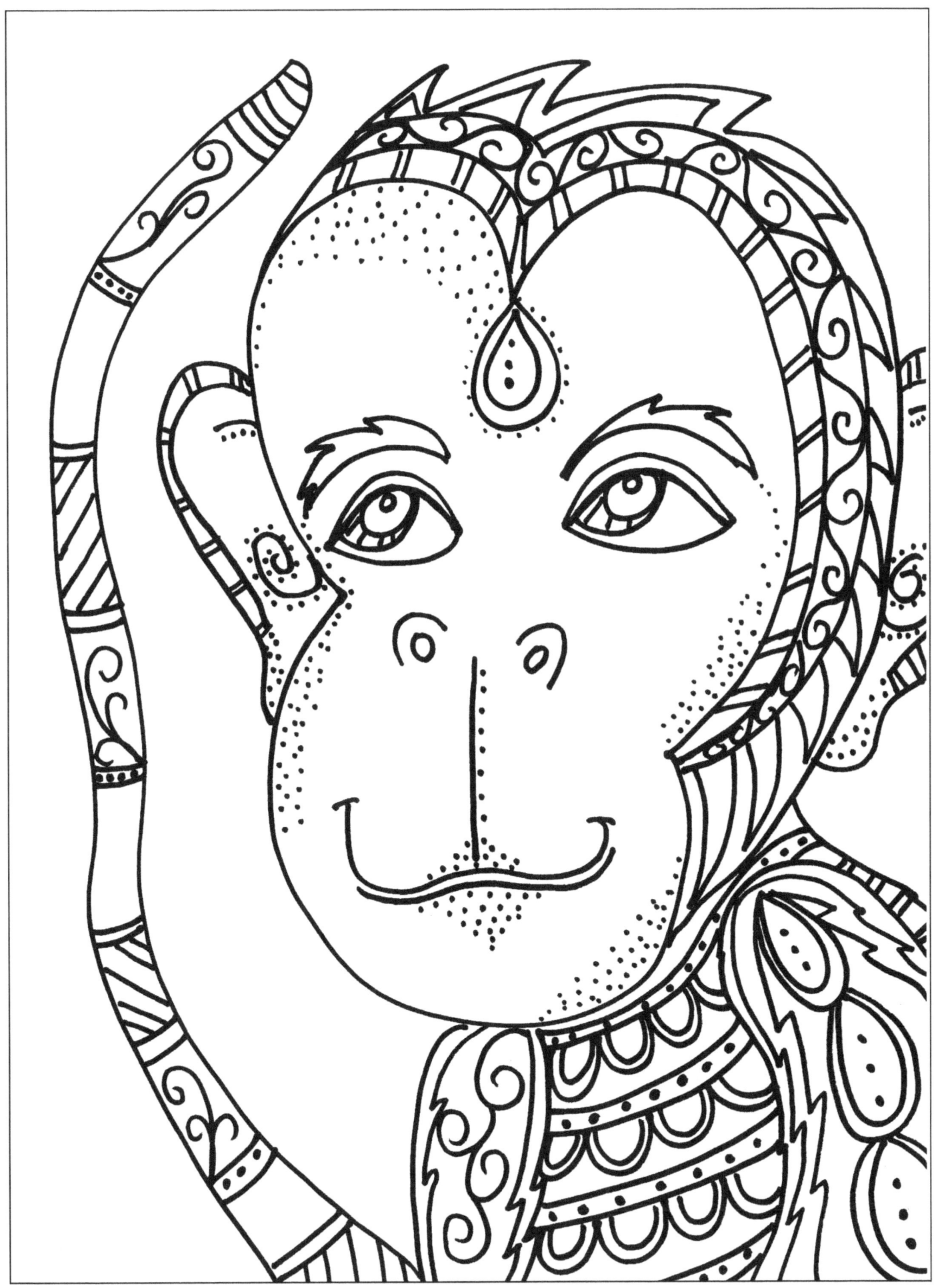

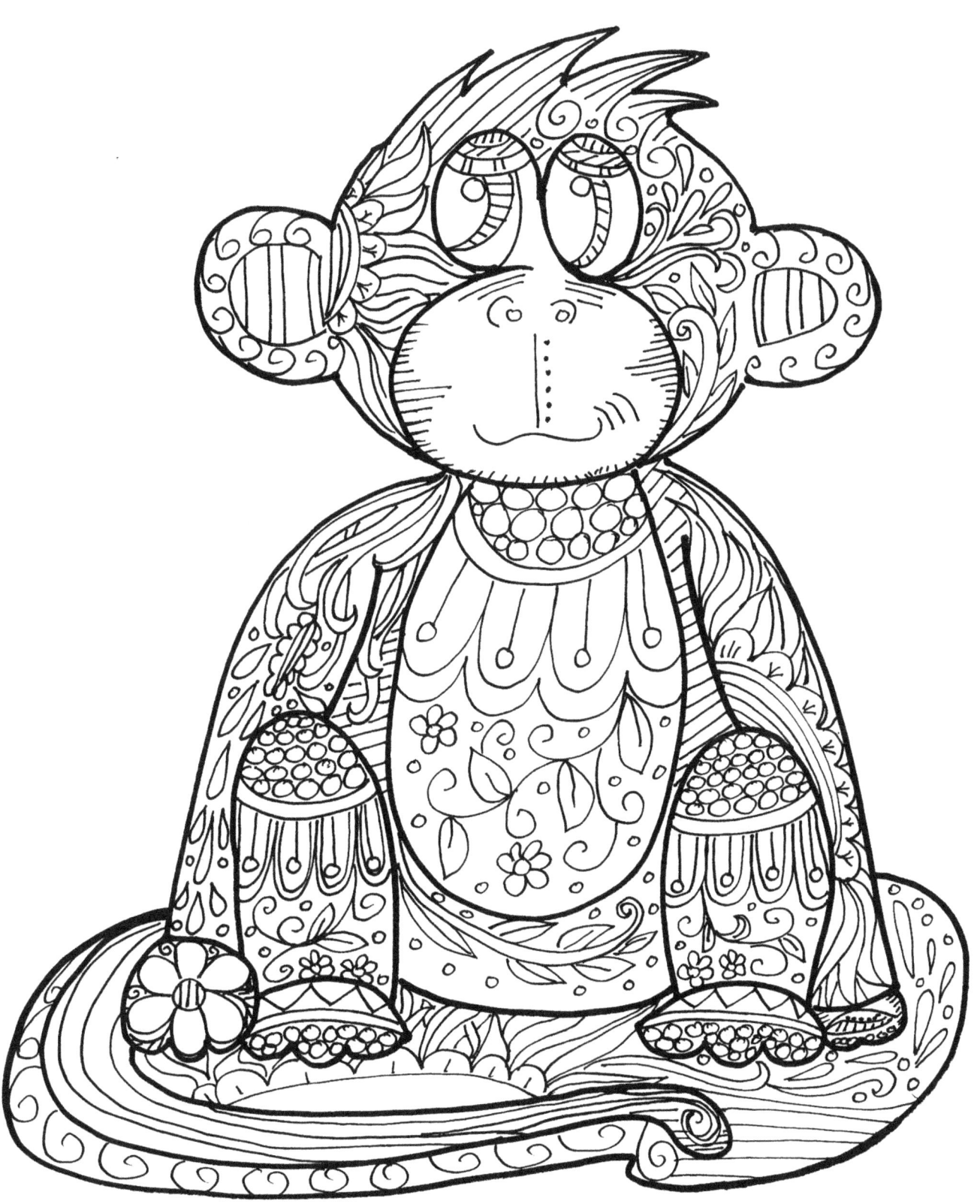

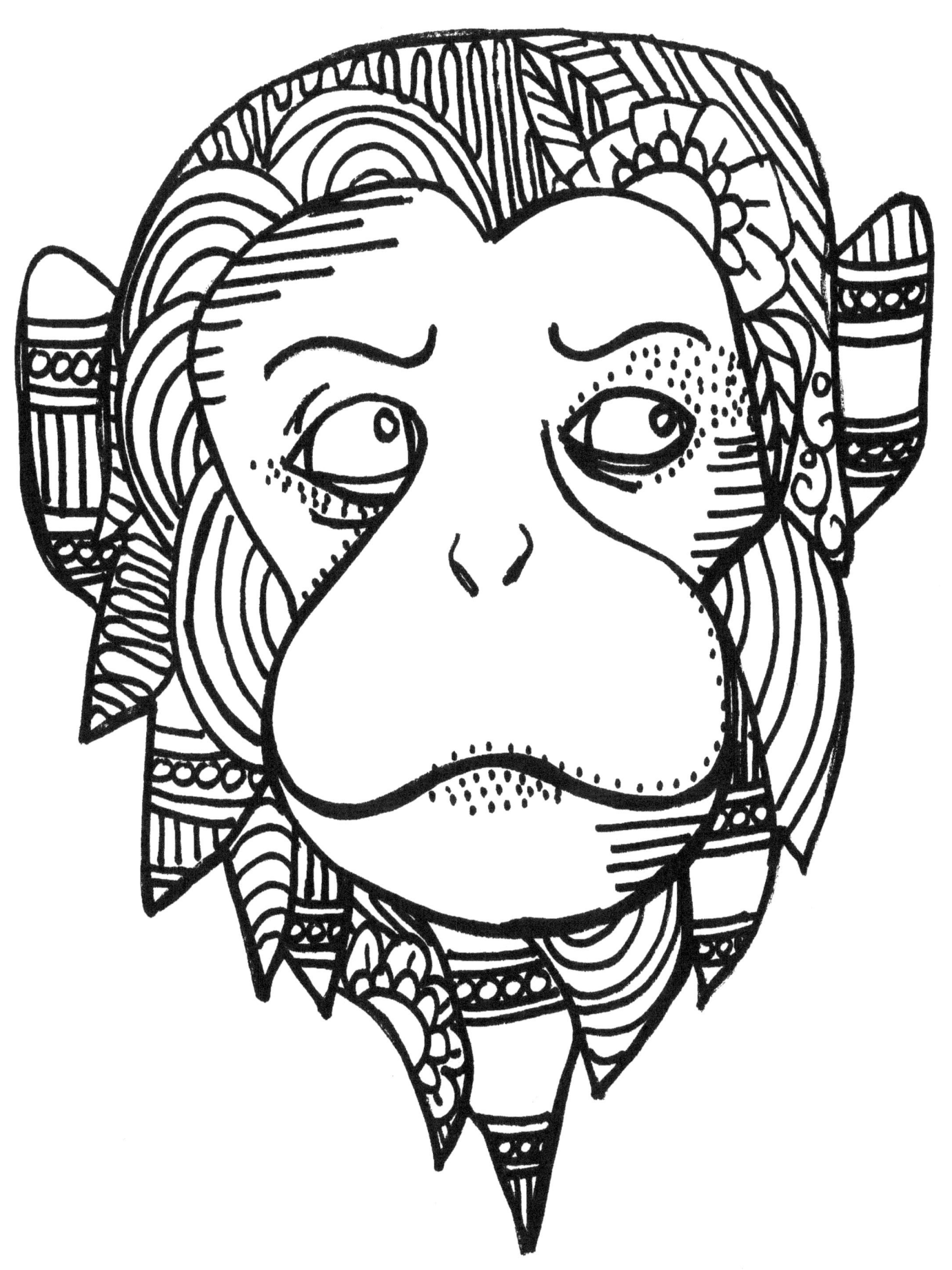

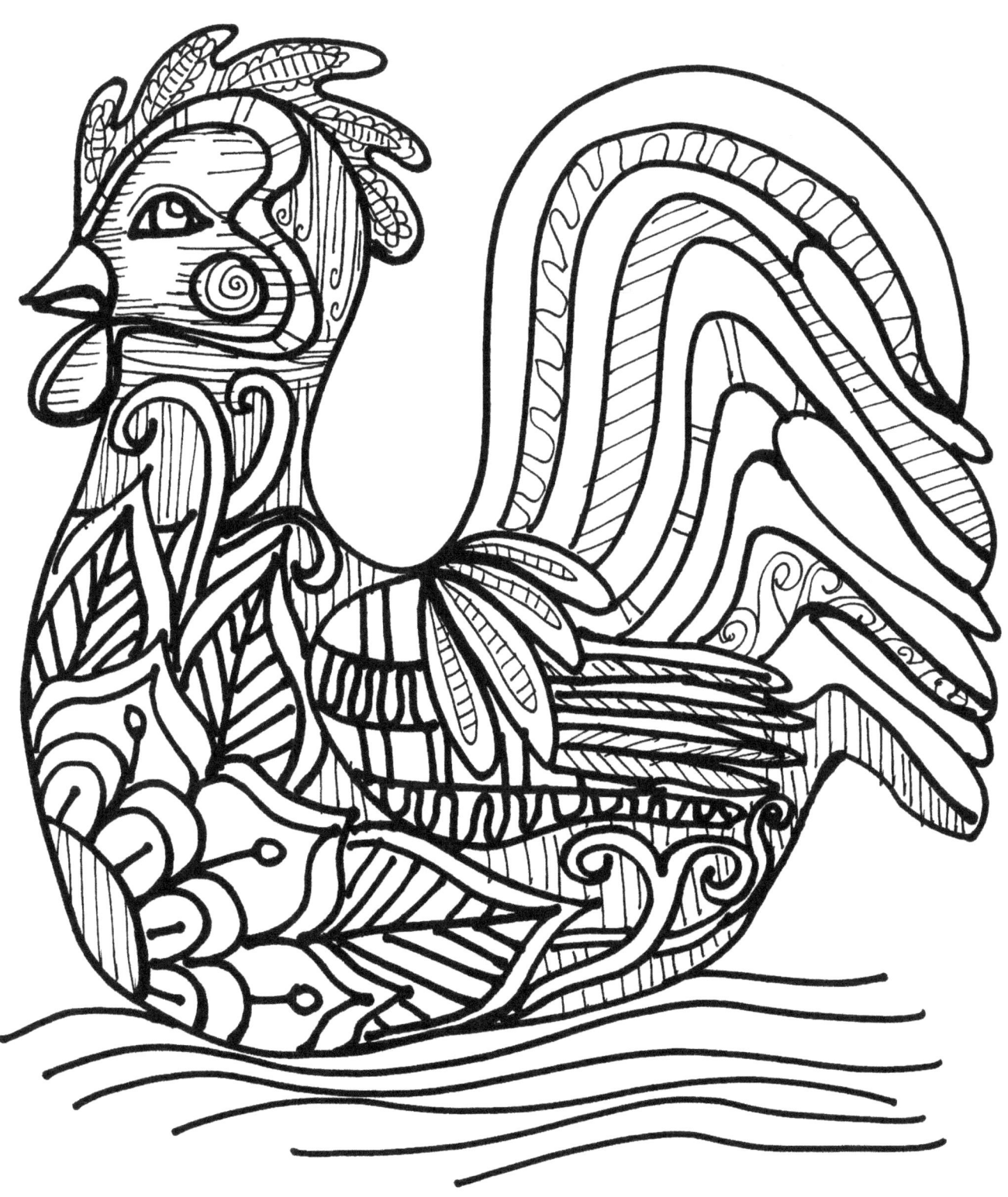

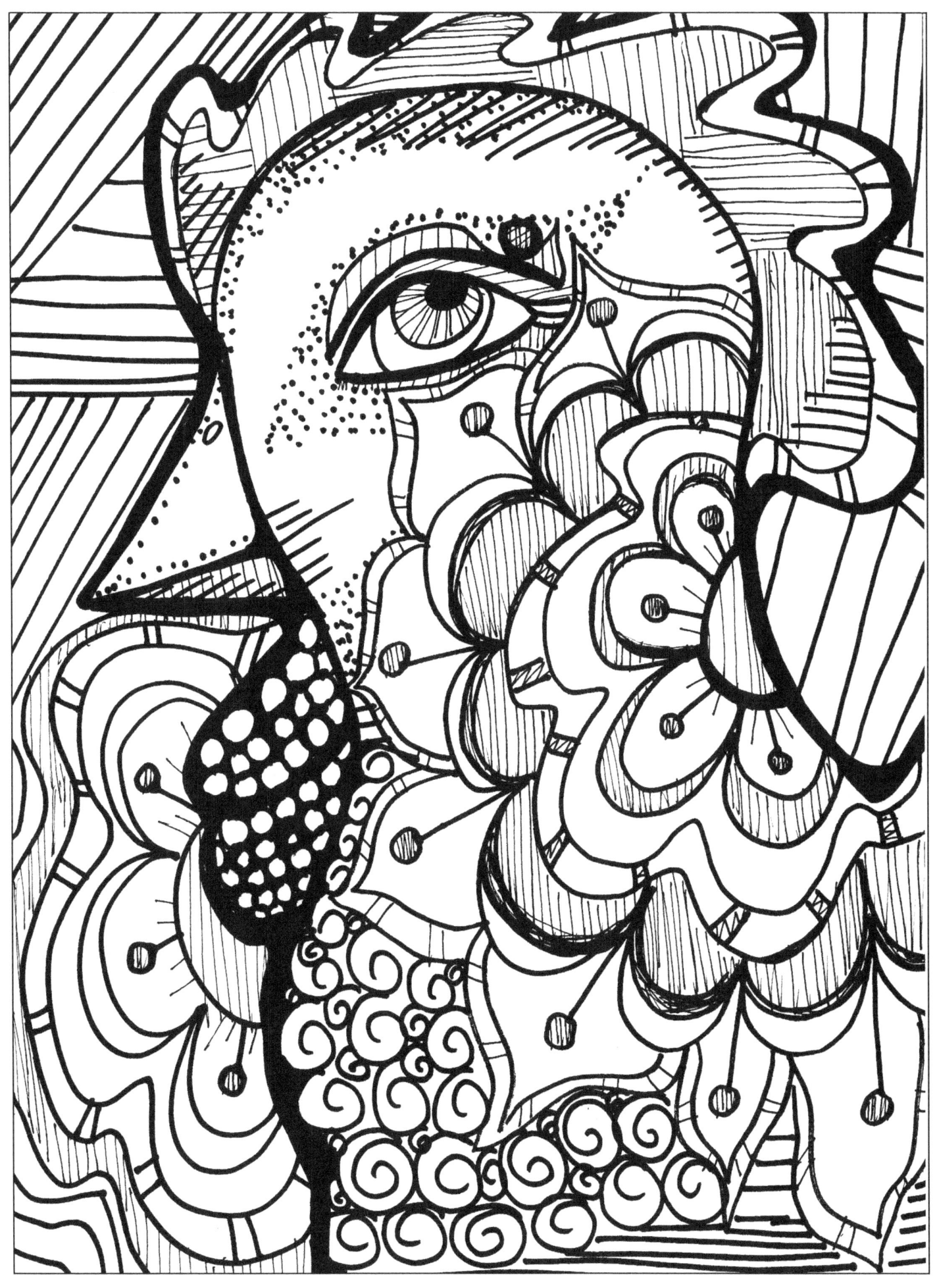

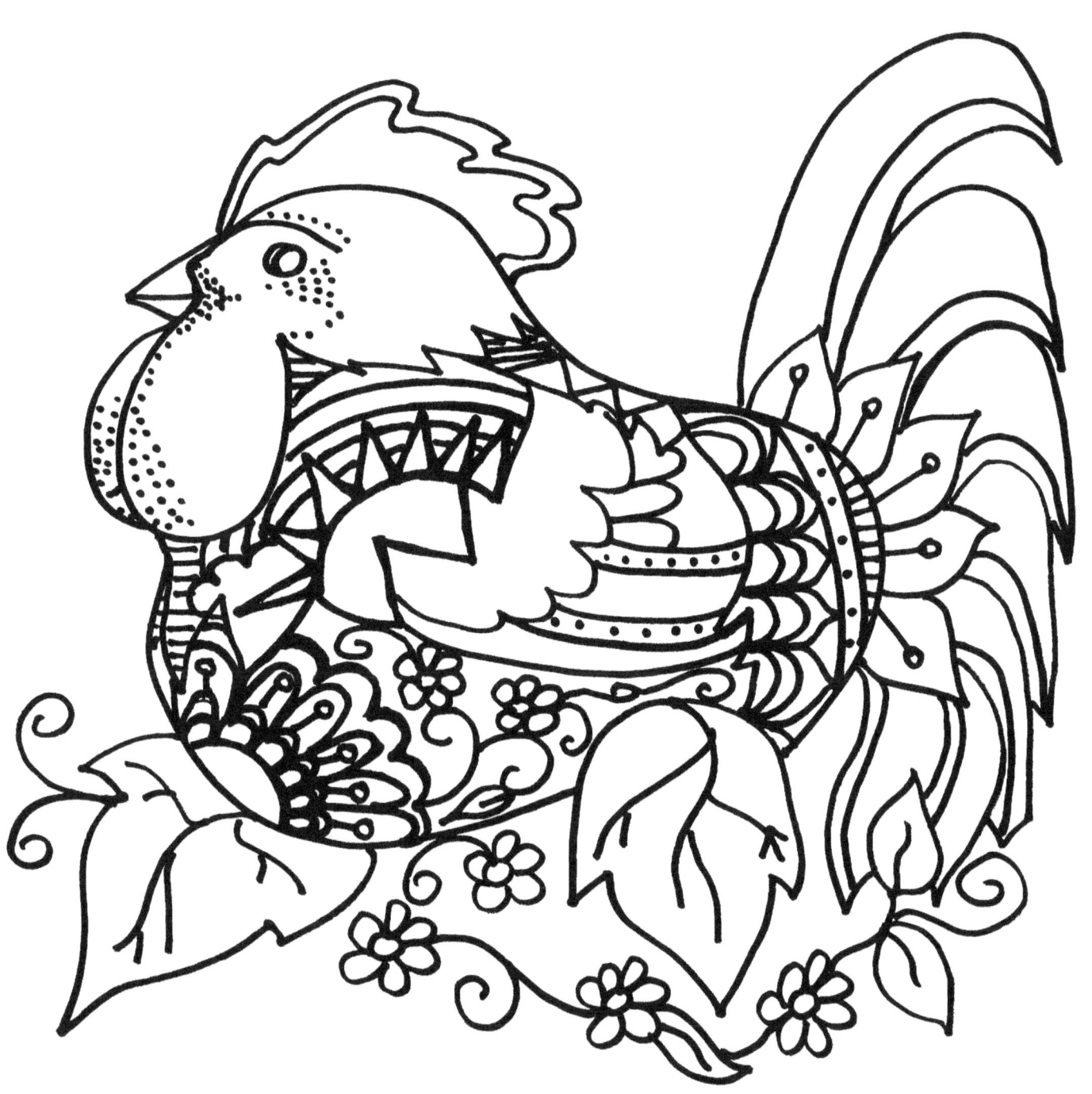

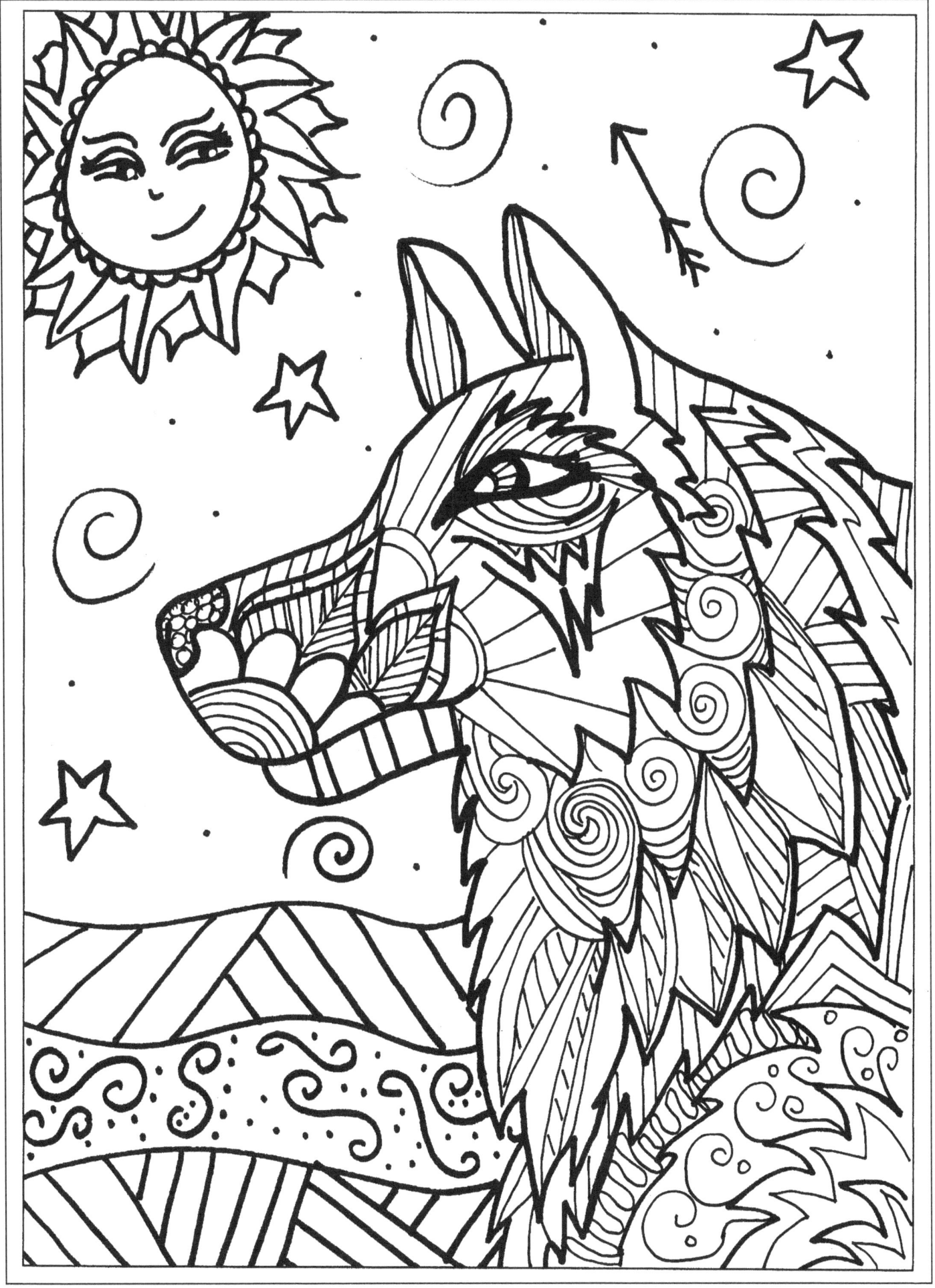

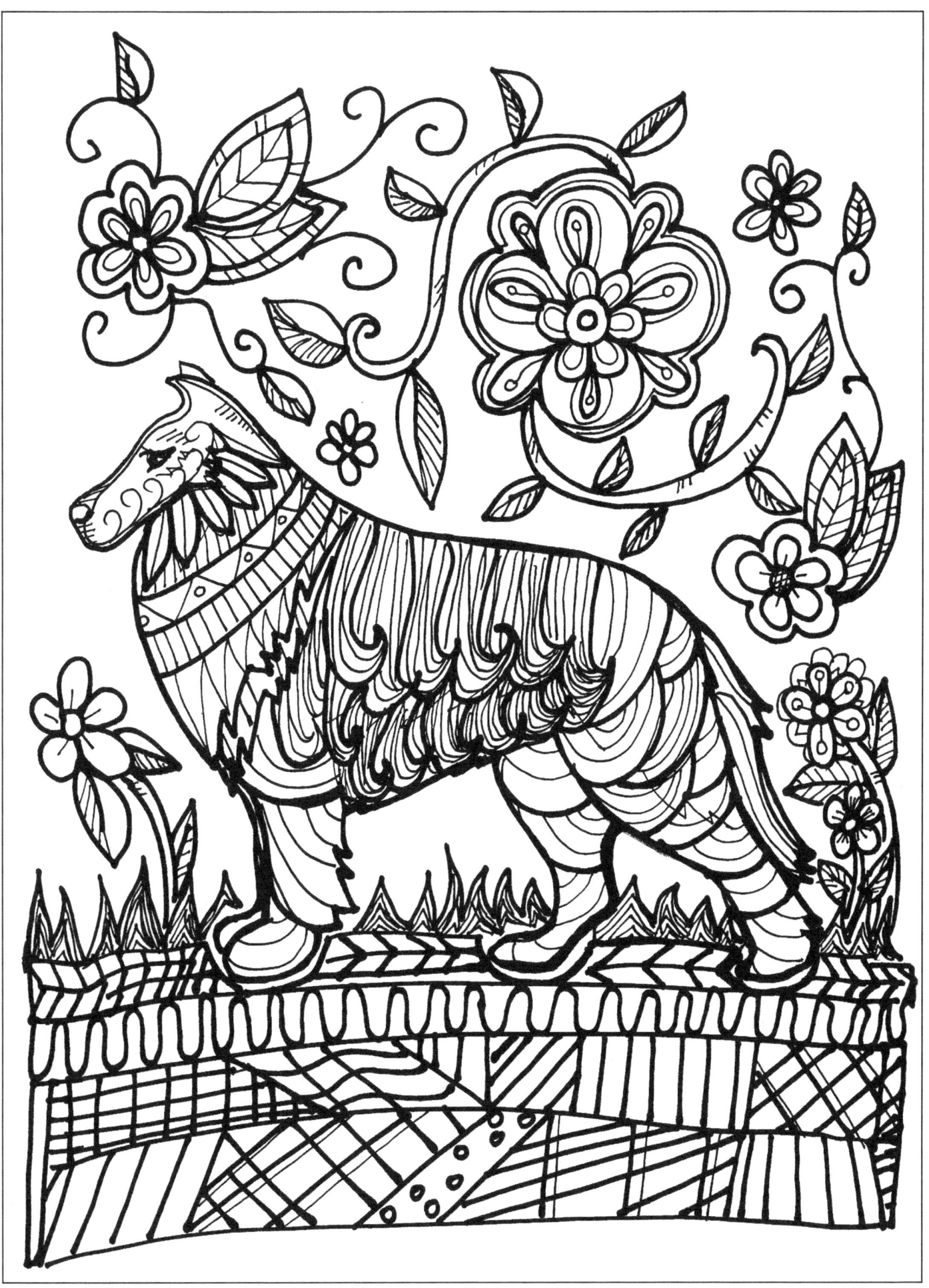

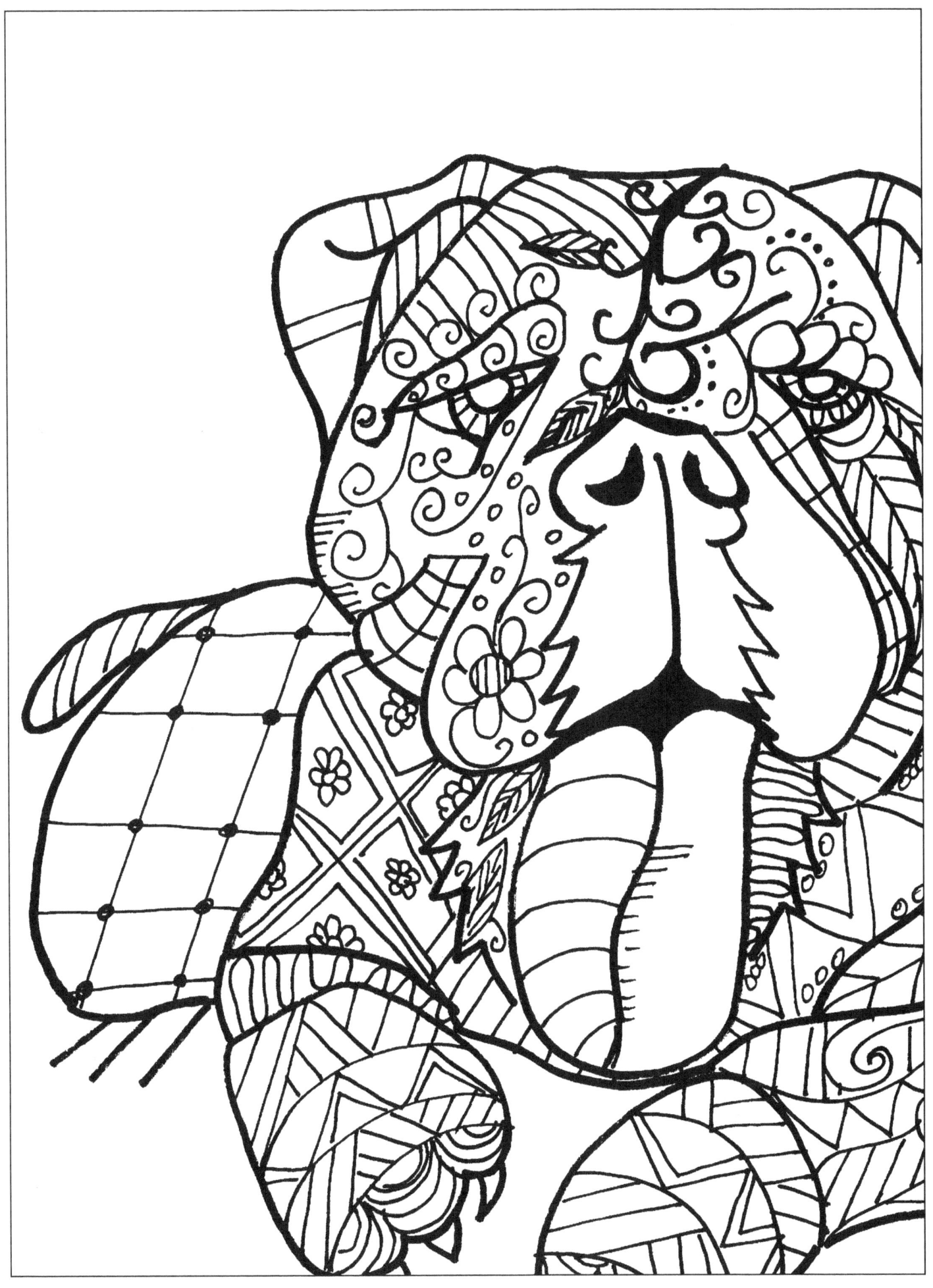

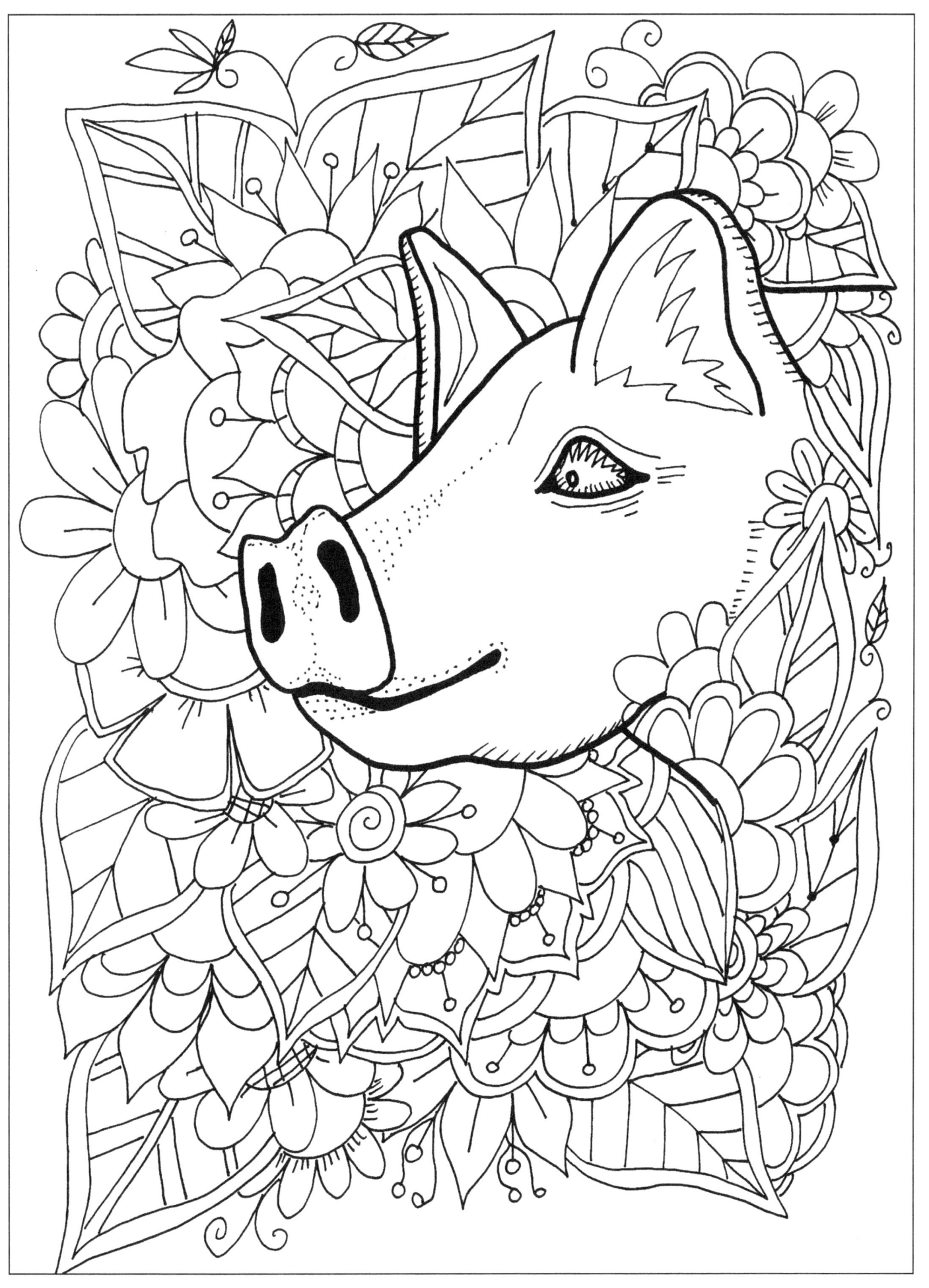

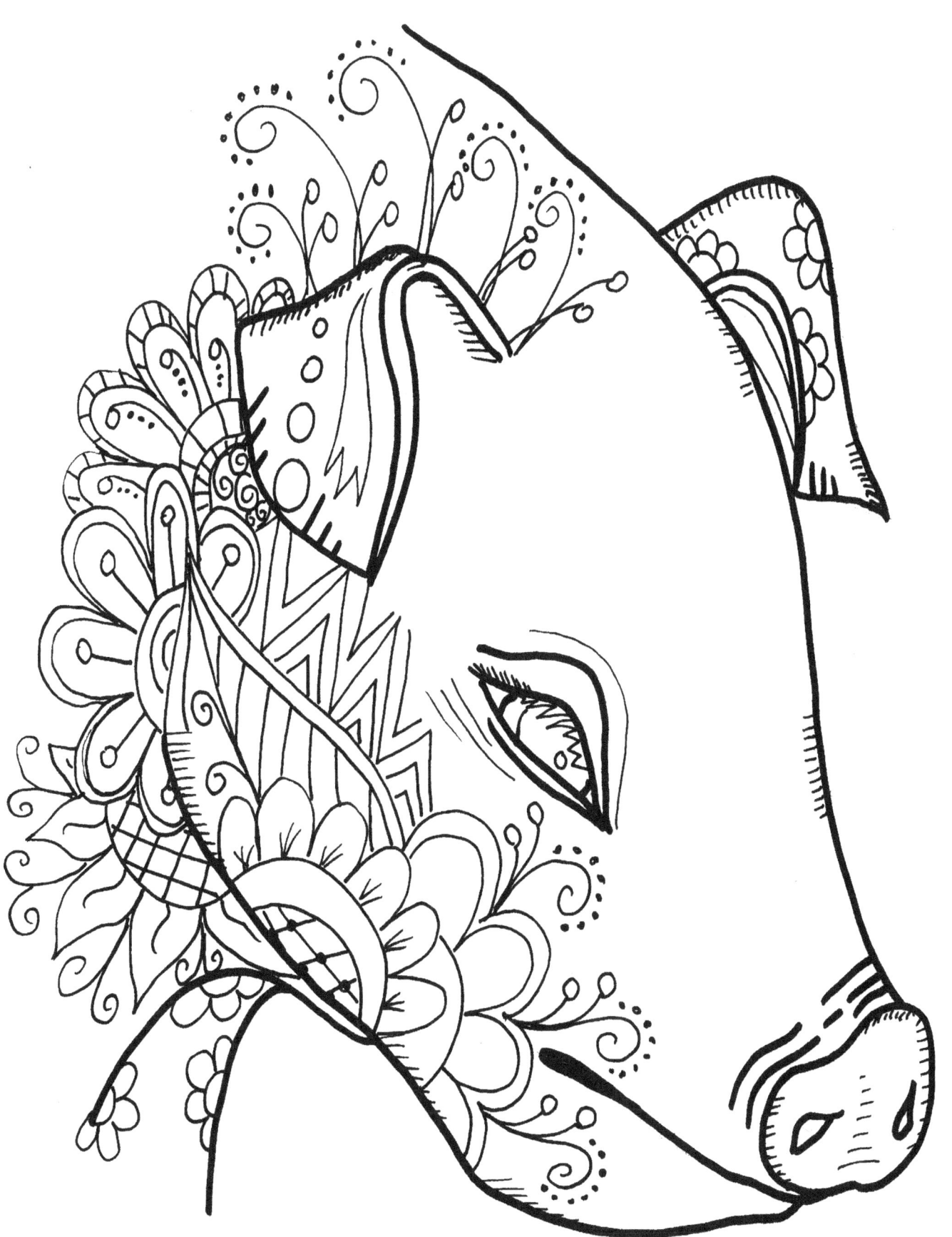

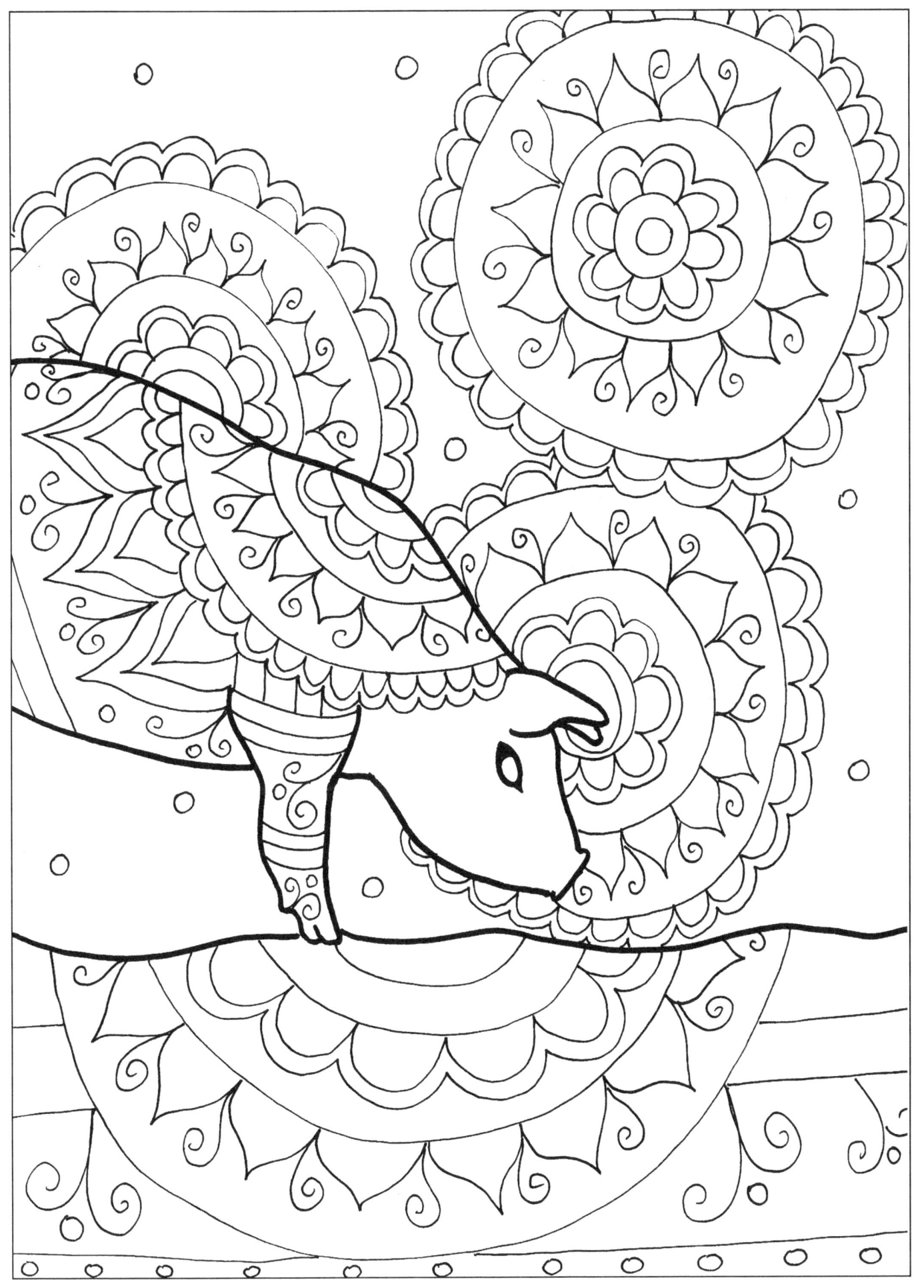

Year of the Rat

People born in the year of the Rat are said to be quick, resourceful and smart. Rats could work on having a broader perspective and learn to have more courage.

The Elements

Wood Rat: Independent, creative, team player

Fire Rat: Brave, gentle, strict, friendly

Earth Rat: Honest, content, adaptable, strong self-esteem

Metal Rat: Smart, motivated, charming, good with money

Water Rat: Talkative, conservative, wise

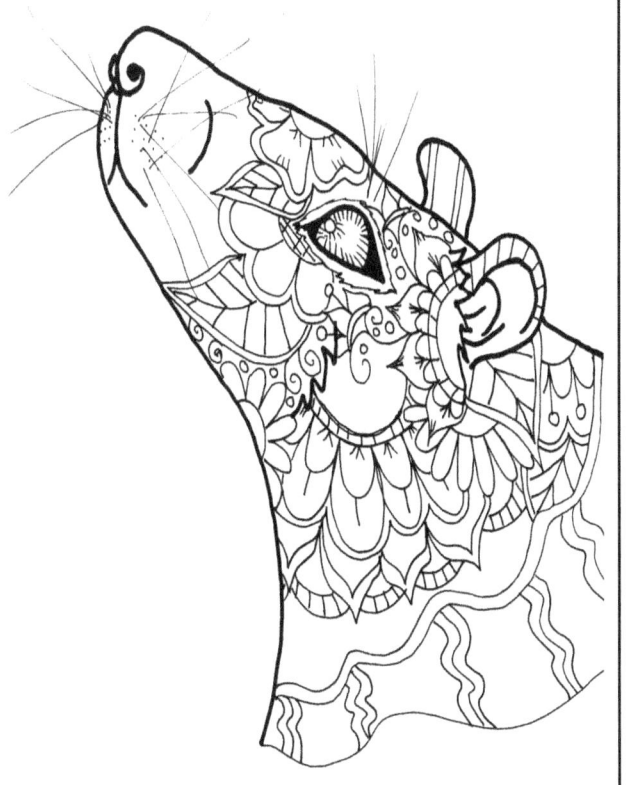

The Basics:

Fixed Season: Winter

Fixed Direction: West/Northwest

Fixed Element: Water

Associated Sun Sign: Sagittarius

Lucky Colour: blue, gold, green

Lucky Numbers: 2, 5, 6

Time of Day: 11pm - 1pm

Compatibility:

Good : Dragon, Rabbit, Ox

Year of the Ox

People born in the year of the Ox are known for their strength, dependability and hard work. Ox people are creative and patient. The Ox could work on being less stubborn and focus on better communication skills.

The Elements

Wood Ox: Brave, restless, outspoken and determined

Fire Ox: Clever, practical, narrow-minded, can be careless

Earth Ox: Smart, confident, responsible, honest

Metal Ox: Busy, active, popular

Water Ox: Hardworking, tireless, careful and ambitious

The Basics:

Fixed Season: Winter

Fixed Direction: North

Fixed Element: Earth

Associated Sun Sign: Capricorn

Lucky Colour: white, blue, purple

Lucky Numbers: 1, 9, 0

Time of Day: 1:00-3:00 am

Compatibility:

Good : Rat, snake, rooster

Bad : sheep, tiger, dragon

Year of the Tiger

People born in the year of the Tiger are said to be strong and stable. They love adventure and discovering new things. Tigers could work on holding less inside and learn how to better deal with stress.

The Elements

Wood Tiger: Compassionate, Level-headed, Good sense of humor

Fire Tiger: Optimistic, Independent, Unpredictable

Earth Tiger: Adventurous, Realistic, faithful but non romantic

Gold Tiger: Enthusiastic, Loyal, Stubborn

Water Tiger: Grounded, Intelligent, Intuitive

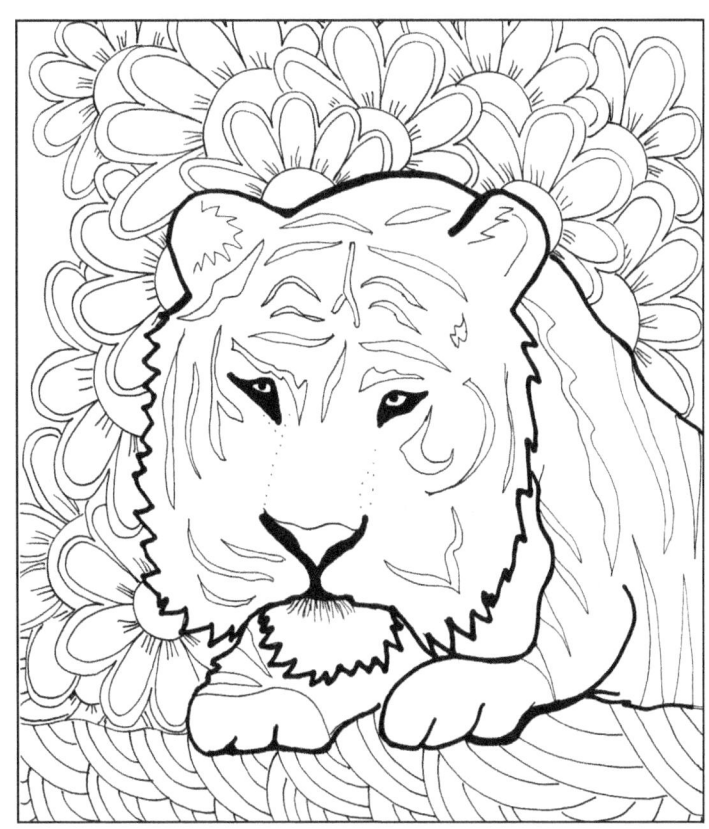

The Basics:

Fixed Season: Spring

Fixed Direction: East-NorthEast

Fixed Element: Wood

Associated Sun Sign: Aquarius

Lucky Colour: blue, grey, white, orange

Lucky Numbers: 1, 3, 4

Time of Day: 3:00am to 5:00am

Compatibility:

Good : Dragon, Horse, Pig

Year of the Rabbit

People born in the year of the Rabbit are said to be gracious and sensitive. They are gentle, quick minded and kind. Rabbits should work toward being less timid and less conservative.

The Elements

Wood Rabbit: Clever, lively and quick-witted.

Fire Rabbit: Can easily see the overall picture, smart and flexible.

Earth Rabbit: Straightforward, hard-working, very reserved

Metal Rabbit: Kind, conservative and enthusiastic

Water Rabbi: Gentle, adjust easily to situations, agreeable

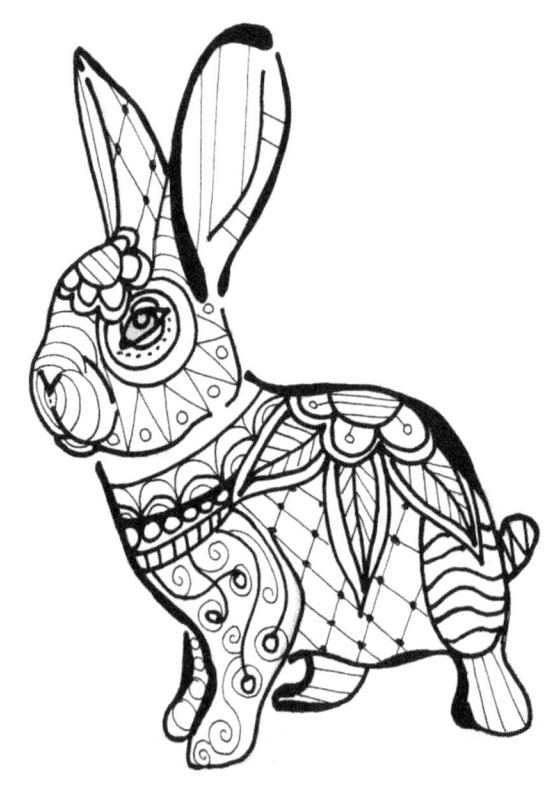

The Basics:

Fixed Season: Spring

Fixed Direction: East

Fixed Element: Wood

Associated Sun Sign: Pisces

Lucky Color: Red, Pink, Purple

Lucky Numbers: 3, 4, 6

Time of Day: 5am - 7an

Compatibility:
Good: Sheep, Monkey, Dog, Pig

Bad: Snake, Rooster

Year of the Dragon

People born in the year of the Dragon are said to be strong with a great ability to love, are ambitious and can realize their dreams. Dragons should work toward being less frustrated and critical of others.

The Elements

Wood Dragon: Introverted, creative, innovative

Fire Dragon: Quick, intelligent, easygoing

Earth Dragon: Smart, grounded, hardworking, supportive

Gold Dragon: Strong, unpredictable emotions, determined

Water Dragon: Intuitive, persevering, farsighted

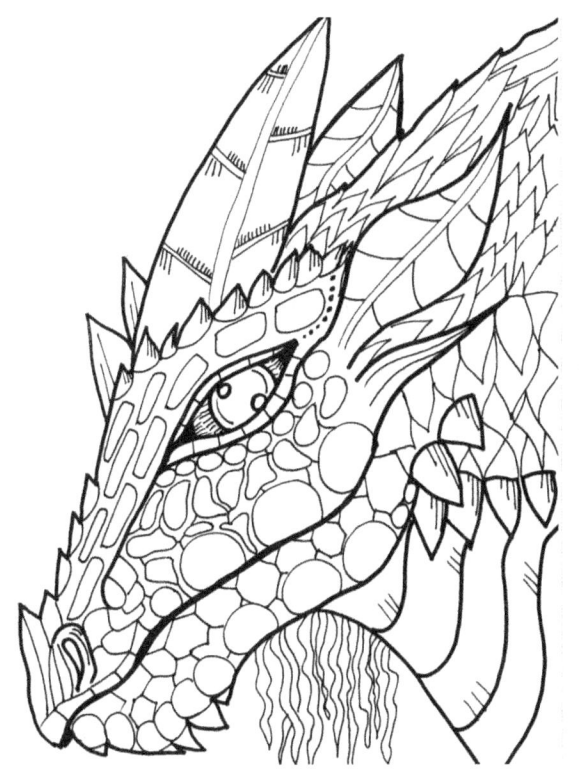

The Basics:

Fixed Season: Spring

Fixed Direction: East

Fixed Element: Earth

Associated Sun Sign: Aries

Lucky Colour: gold, silver, grey

Lucky Numbers: 1, 6, 7

Time of Day: 7:00-9:00am

Compatibility:

Good : Snake, Rat, Tiger

Bad : Dog, Goat, Ox

Year of the Snake

People born in the year of the Snake are said to be smart, funny and creative. Passionate and warm hearted they are easily trusted. Snakes should work toward staying relaxed and taking time out to restore themselves.

The Elements

Wood Snake: Neat, good taste, easy going

Fire Snake: Intelligent, quick-minded, charming, social

Earth Snake: Quick, loyal, sensitive, kind

Metal Snake: Good willpower, courageous, down to earth

Water Snake: Optimistic, adventurous, creative, artistic

The Basics:

Fixed Season: Summer

Fixed Direction: South, Southeast

Fixed Element: Fire

Associated Sun Sign: Taurus

Lucky Colour: red, black, yellow

Lucky Numbers: 2, 8, 9

Time of Day: 9:00-11:00 am

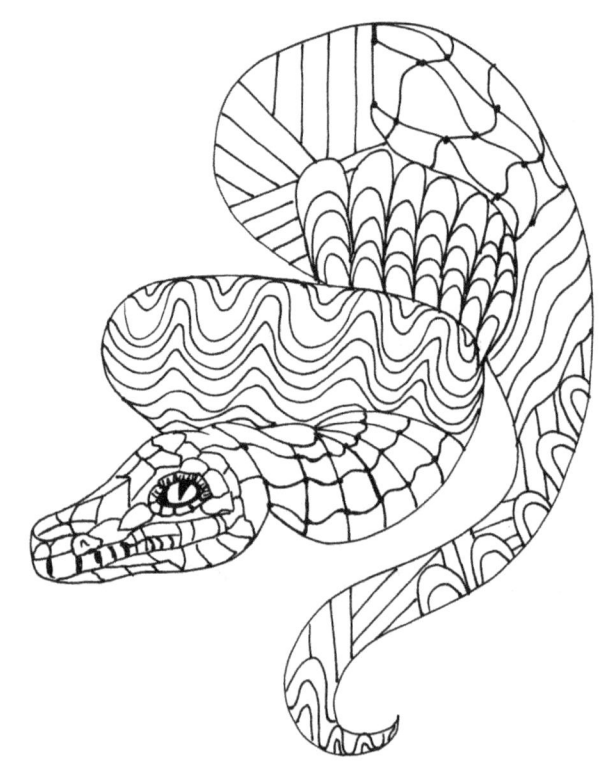

Compatibility:

Good : Ox, Pig

Bad : Rat, Monkey, Rooster

Year of the Horse

People born in the year of the Horse are said to be flexible and loyal friends. They are easy going, independent and usually have a positive attitude. Horses could work on being less stubborn and more persistent.

The Elements

Wood Horse: Good leader, decision maker, imaginative, opinionated

Fire Horse: Intelligent, passionate, very energetic and sensitive

Earth Horse: Optimistic, grounded, practical

Metal Horse: Active, enjoys challenge, stubborn

Water Horse: Cheerful, intuitive, easily distracted

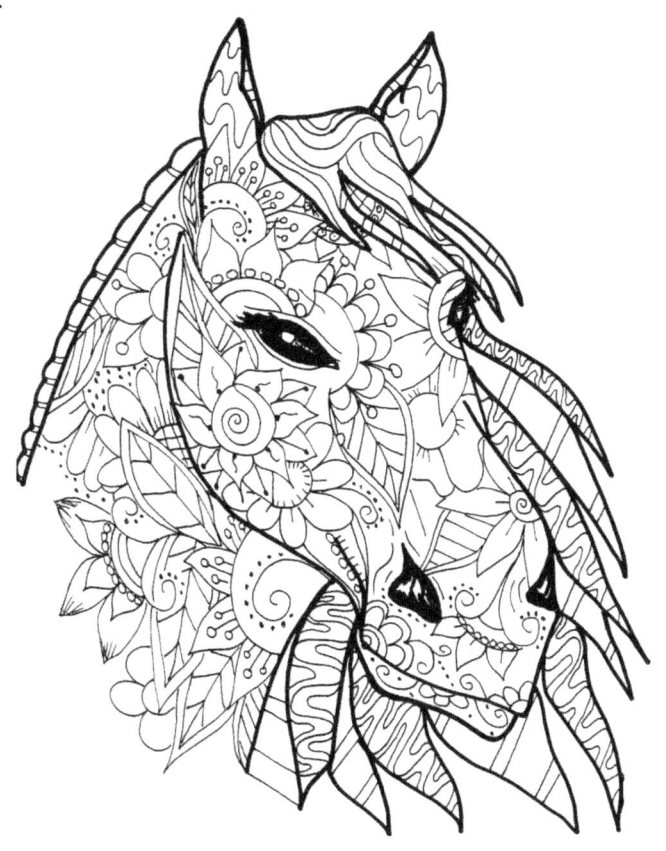

The Basics:

Fixed Season: Summer

Fixed Direction: South

Fixed Element: Fire

Associated Sun Sign: Gemini

Lucky Colour: brown, yellow, purple

Lucky Numbers: 2, 3, 7

Time of Day: 11am-1pm

Compatibility:
Good : Tiger, Sheep, Dog,

Year of the Goat (Sheep or Ram)

People born in the year of the Goat (Sheep or Ram) are said to be gentle, wise and full of compassion. They are resilient, reserved and quiet . The Goat (Sheep or Ram) could work on being less hasty and shy.

The Elements

Wood Goat: Gentle, kind and polite, compassionate.

Fire Goat: Loyal and honest, love having their surroundings clean and tidy.

Earth Goat: Honest and straightforward, enjoy spending time with friends.

Metal Goat: Ambitious, responsible, stubborn, act in good faith.

Water Goat: Talented, willing to help others, respected, stable

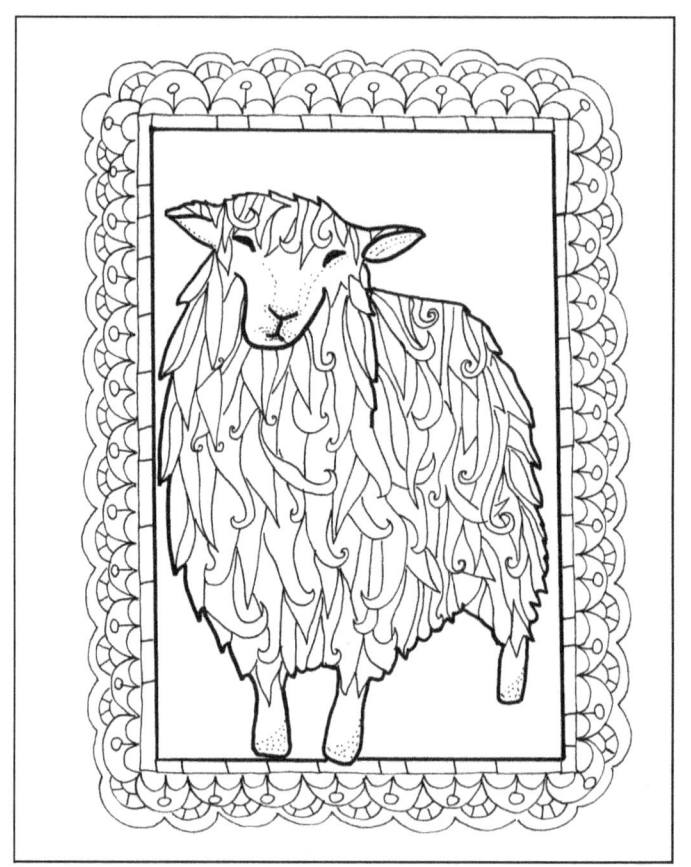

The Basics:

Fixed Season: Summer

Fixed Direction: South/Southwest

Fixed Element: Earth

Associated Sun Sign: Cancer

Lucky Colour: Green, Red, Purple

Lucky Numbers: 6, 7, 8

Time of Day: 1:00pm - 3:00pm

Compatibility:

Good : Horse, Rabbit, Pig

Bad : Ox, Tiger, Dog

Year of the Monkey

People born in a Monkey Year are said to be playful, curious and creative. They tend to be kind and have a good attitude. They do however need to develop patience and learn to listen others ideas.

The Elements

Fire Monkey: Ambitious, strong, adventurous

Wood Monkey: Like to help others, compassionate, good communicators

Water Monkey: Sensitive, quick-witted, jokester

Metal Monkey: Smart, determined, ambitious, quick-witted, likeable

Earth Monkey: Dependable, optimistic, go-getter

The Basics

Fixed Season : Autumn Fixed

Fixed Direction : West-Southwest

Fixed Element : Metal / Yang Associated Sun

Associated Sun Sign : Leo

Time of day: 3pm - 5pm

Lucky Colours: white, gold, blue

Lucky Numbers: 3, 7, 9

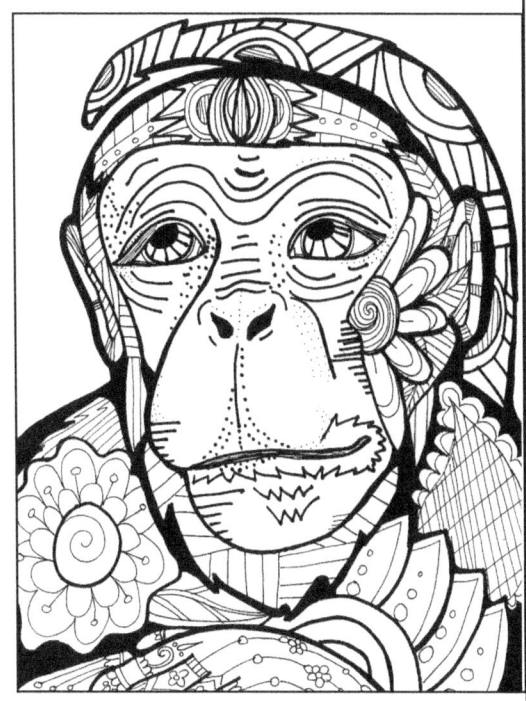

Compatibility

Good: Dragon, Rat, Rooster

Bad: Tiger, Snake

Year of the Rooster

People born in a Rooster Year are said to be honest, full of ambition and are great at communication. They are independent and enthusiastic. They need to however develop faith and patience.

The Elements

Wood Rooster: Energetic, easy going, tender, kind, thoughtful

Fire Rooster: Trustworthy, independent, proud, responsible, courageous

Earth Rooster: Lovely, persistent, calm, generous, trustworthy, motivated

Metal Rooster: Determined, realistic, brave, frank, strong will power, hardworking

Water Rooster: Smart, quick-witted, quiet, peaceful, compassionate

The Basics:

Fixed Season : Autumn

Fixed Direction : West

Fixed Element : Metal / Yin

Associated Sun Sign : Virgo

Lucky Color : Black, Yellow Brown, Gold, Brown

Lucky Numbers : 1, 2, 6, 8

Time of Day: 5pm—7pm

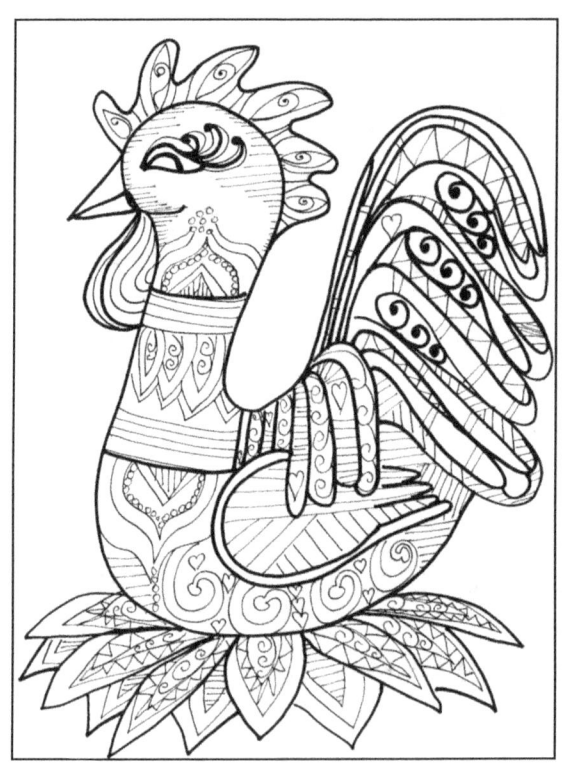

Compatibility:

Good : Ox, Snake

Bad : Rat, Rabbit, Horse, Rooster, Dog

Year of the Dog

People born in the year of the Dog are said to be loyal and honest. They are kind and good listeners. Dogs are good natured, good friends and often shy. Dogs need to learn to relax and be less stubborn.

The Elements

Wood Dog: Sincere, trustworthy, considerate, understanding and patient

Fire Dog: Intelligent, hardworking, and sincere

Earth Dog: Good communicator, serious, responsible

Metal Dog: Conservative, cautious and service oriented

Water Dog: Brave, self-centered, good with finances

The Basics:

Fixed Season : Autumn

Fixed Direction : South, East

Fixed Element : Metal

Associated Sun Sign : Libra

Lucky Color : Green, Red, Purple

Lucky Numbers : 3, 4, 9

Time of Day: 7pm-9pm

Compatibility:
Good: Rabbit, Horse, Tiger

Bad: Dragon, Goat, Rooster

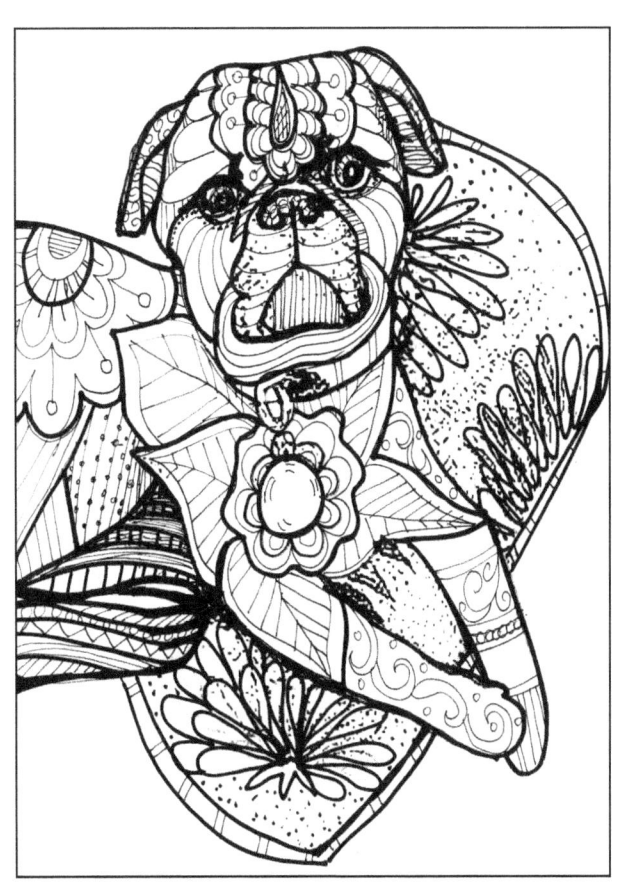

Year of the Pig

People born in the year of the Pig are said to be gentle and enjoy spending time with others. Pigs are easy going, honest and sincere. Pigs could work on following their dreams and learn to ask for help when needed.

The Elements

Wood Pig: Honest, Easygoing, carefree, good communicator

Fire Pig: Good leaders, optimistic, cooperative, ambitions

Earth Pig: Grounded, patient, thoughtful

Metal Pig: Gentle, affectionate, caring

Water Pig: Responsible, intuitive, peaceful

The Basics:

Fixed Season: Winter

Fixed Direction: North-Northwest

Fixed Element: Water

Associated Sun Sign: Scorpio

Lucky Colour: yellow, grey, brown, gold

Lucky Numbers: 2, 5, 8

Time of Day: 9 pm - 11 pm

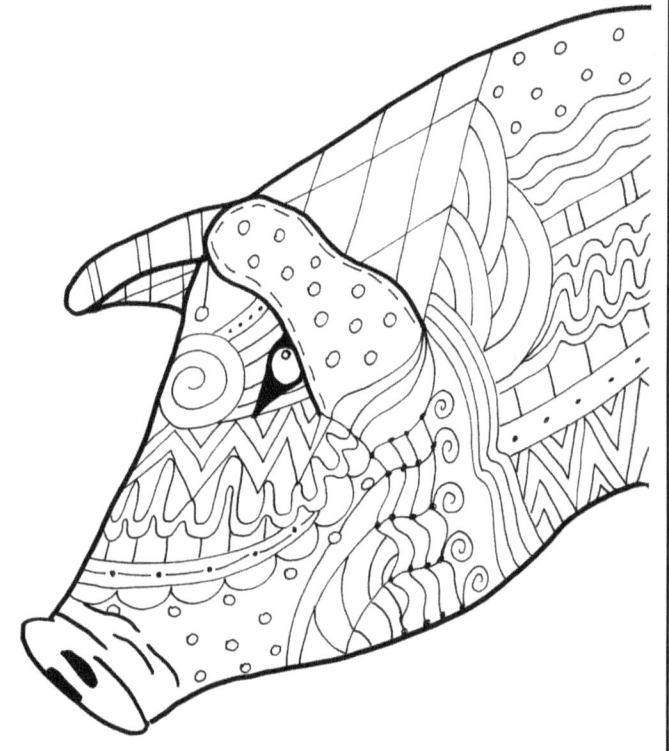

Compatibility:

Good : Tiger, Rabbit, Sheep

Bad : Snake, Monkey

Chinese Zodiac Meditation

You could have someone read this to you slowly, record yourself and play it back or read it through and follow the process. You may choose to lie down or remain seated; whatever you decide allow yourself to be comfortable.

Let's begin to notice the largest sensation of breath in the body.

Allow this breath to expand to include the entire body.

Imagine sending your breath from the top of your head down to the tips of your toes. And as you breath softy and gently you invite yourself to relax.

Relax the scalp and crown of the head…..

Relax your shoulders back and down from the ears…...

Relax the upper cheeks, lower cheeks, jaw and tongue. Give the whole face permission to soften even further now…...

Relax your ears…...

Relax the neck…...

Relax the shoulders back and down, if seated, allow the elbows to dangle from the shoulder girdle. If lying down allow the elbows to relax…...

Let the hands relax, fingers releasing to their natural curve…...

Feel the breath rising and falling in the chest…...

Feel the abdomen expand and collapse with the breath…...

Let these sensations drop into the back side of the body and release the vertebrae; each one in turn from the cervical spine in the neck all the way down to the sacrum and coccyx…...

Allow the hips to relax…...

Release any tension in the thighs, your knees, the lower legs, ankles and feet…...

Let any remaining tension release from the body from the tips of the toes……

So relaxed from the top of the head all the way down to the tips of the toes……

Any sounds you hear allow you to sink even deeper into a state of rest, of relaxation. Let go. Let it all go now as you invite your body to rest.

Bring the focus to the belly button area and using your mind's eye see, sense, feel or imagine yourself outdoors.

This can be any place outside that you enjoy; by a river or stream, in an open field or a shaded forest. Be anywhere in your mind you believe your Zodiac animal would inhabit.

And give this outdoor space as much detail as you wish:

What do you see here?

What do you hear?

What do you smell?

Enliven all of your senses.

Find a place to sit down in this outdoor space; somewhere comfortable. As you come to a state of further rest, of relaxation, invite your Zodiac Animal to come to you. Invite it in using whatever words you choose.

Then continue to sit and wait.

The animal comes….. possibly from your right or left, maybe from above or from behind.

When it shows itself notice all of the qualities of the animal:

Does it tend to be fast or slow?

Is it dull or brilliant?

Is it large or small?

What kinds of sounds does it make?

See, sense, feel or imagine it fully before you; allow it to come to you so clearly that if you were to open your eyes it would be as if it were standing or lying in front of you.

Take as much time as you need.

Next reflect on the nature of this animal. In particular: what are its strengths?

How easily can it survive?

Is it easy for it to find food, shelter?

What makes this animal thrive?

What traits is this animal best known for?

(You may wish to write these answers down.)

How could these traits apply to your life? How can you, holding this animal as your personal Zodiac, deepen your experience? How could you use its talents to enhance your journey?

Ask the animal what it can teach you and listen to what it has to share.

Sit and be with the animal for as much time as you wish: maybe go for a walk with it and as you share space with this being.
Listen… (5-15 minutes)

Ask any questions you may have for clarification if needed to receive further understanding. If no further information comes through know you are

 (3-5 minutes of silence)

Thank the animal for sharing space with you. And return to the awareness to the present moment; knowing you can find your Zodiac animal whenever you choose as they are deeply connected with your heart.

Slowly now bring your awareness back to the physical body.

Notice the breath. Allow your breathing to slow and deep and even.

Notice the physical sensations of relaxation in the body. And give yourself permission to carry with you as much of these relaxed feelings you may need as you continue into your day.

Take a long slow and full breathe and imagine sending your breath from the top of your head down to the tips of your toes.

Breathe from the top of your head to the knees.

Breathe from the top of your head down to your root (the groin area).

Breathe in from the top of your head down to the navel.

Breathe in from the top of the head heart center.

Breathe in from the top of the head to the throat center.

Breathe in from the top of the head to your eyes.

Slowly begin to wiggle the fingers and toes.

Open the eyes when you feel ready.

Continue along with your day knowing you have a strong connection with your Zodiac Animal. It wishes you much luck, peace and prosperity.

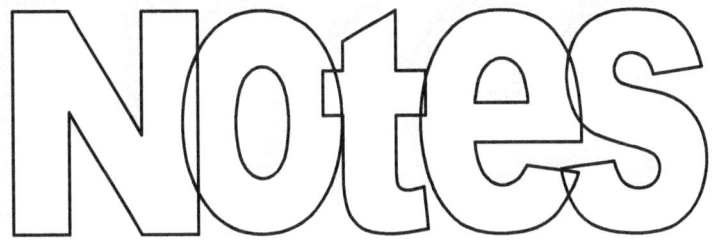

Birthdays

Rat	Ox	Tiger	Rabbit

Dragon	Snake	Horse	Ram/Sheep/Goat

Monkey	Rooster	Dog	Pig

About the Creator:

Tammy Lawrence-Cymbalisty is an Alternative Care provider working in the Kitchener/Waterloo Region. Since 2001 she has helped many people find peace, happiness, harmony and further purpose in their lives.

Tammy holds many degrees including: B.A. Sociology (Trent University), Certified Yoga Teacher, Reiki Master/Teacher, HypnoBirthing® Practitioner, Meditation Teacher, Workshop facilitator, Writer, Personal Growth Coach.

She lives with her husband, two felines and a school of fins in Cambridge, ON and is a Monkey in the Chinese Zodiac.

Find out more by following Tammy on social media:

http://www.twitter.com/tllc

http://www.tinyurl.com/tlcservices

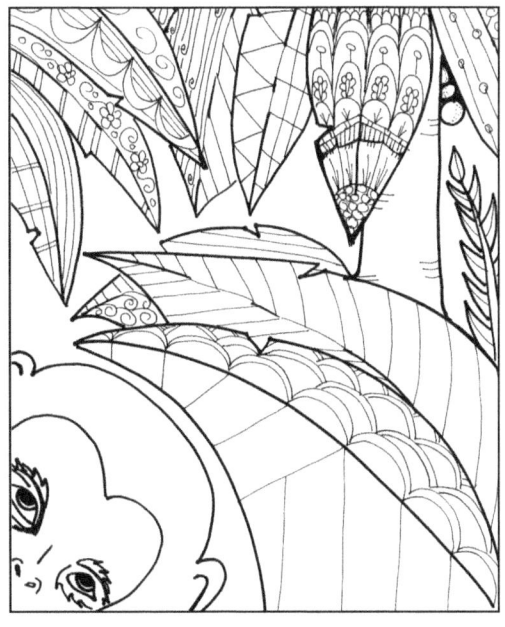

May you find peace

May you find happiness

May you be free from suffering

Namaste, Tammy

Be sure to purchase other colouring books designed & created by me! Visit my Author Page: https://goo.gl/e387qf

www.ingramcontent.com/pod-product-compliance
Lightning Source LLC
Chambersburg PA
CBHW081548240526
45470CB00024B/2704